THE FULLER PICTURE

THE FULLER PICTURE

Cam Fuller Looks at Life

CAM FULLER

 FriesenPress

Suite 300 - 990 Fort St
Victoria, BC, V8V 3K2
Canada

www.friesenpress.com

Copyright © 2020 by Cam Fuller
First Edition — 2020

ISBN
978-1-5255-5907-5 (Hardcover)
978-1-5255-5908-2 (Paperback)
978-1-5255-5909-9 (eBook)

1. HUMOR, TOPIC, MARRIAGE & FAMILY

Distributed to the trade by The Ingram Book Company

For Us

Contents

Everything changes; nothing is lost.

Foreword

Here, at last, is Cam's book. He'd worked at it off-and-on for a few years – sorting through his columns to find his favourites, the ones he was really proud of and felt worthy of publishing in a book. He had narrowed down his choices, decided how he wanted to organize them and written introductions to the chapters.

After he died in December 2018, I wanted to finish what he had started. I discovered the number of columns he had picked would have made for a very long book, which means some good ones couldn't be included. They're still waiting for their moment in the spotlight.

As Cam's wife, reading and editing his work was a labour of love. It was heart wrenching at times, but Cam's sense of humour and his spot-on observations still made me laugh, just like they always had. And there were many times when I paused to marvel at how he could convey so much with just a few well-chosen words.

I could hear his voice. I felt closer to him. And now you hold the result of his vision – with a few finishing touches added.

This wouldn't have been possible without Heather Persson, Cam's editor at the StarPhoenix. I appreciate her support and that of Postmedia, which provided permission to publish this collection.

Thanks to everyone who cheered me on over these past months – my boys, and family and friends who invariably said, "Oh, that's a good idea!"

when I told them I was going to publish the manuscript Cam had worked so hard on.

Love you, Hon. Hope you like how it turned out.

Donella Hoffman
November 2019

Introduction

The Reason I'm Bothering You

I hate to interrupt, but I'm starting this book. I know, I know, there are lots of books – too many, in fact. Don't blame me. For years and years, I tried not to write any books at all. I was fabulously successful.

You'd be surprised how easy it is to not write a book. In my case, I busied myself by writing for a newspaper. Newspapers are like books but the pages are bigger and you don't feel like a Bond villain when you burn them.

For years and years, everything I've written, every keystroke, every finger tap, every delete and backspace, has happened on company time. I don't actually know how real writers do it. I can only assume they spend their days at home looking out the window at the falling leaves without being interrupted by a police scanner or an overstimulated photographer. Between paroxysms of inspiration, perhaps they tie fashionable sweaters around their necks and go for long walks on sun-dappled boulevards.

Or maybe they inhabit coffee shops where they read books written by other writers. I never learned how to loiter in a coffee shop. And I'm not much of a sweater guy. Thus, by my own definition, I've spent years writing, without ever being a writer.

Until now, he wrote. (And then tossed a stylish mini-paragraph onto the page).

The work day is over. It's dark outside. But instead of doing something productive like sorting drill bits in the garage, I am – dare I say it? – writing. It's like a painter coming home and painting.

My dad was a painter, by the way. Not canvas – drywall. I worked for him in the summer as a student and then full-time after getting my English degree from the University of Saskatchewan in the late 1900s. They called him Stormin' Norman on job sites. His training technique wasn't exactly nurturing. You knew you were doing it right when he wasn't giving you hell. One of our jobs was painting a suite in a high-rise overlooking the StarPhoenix building in downtown Saskatoon. As I put my Arts and Sciences training to work applying beige eggshell latex to a window frame, I looked down at that pale brick building and realized I would work there someday. Somehow, I just knew it.

I wrote a letter to my favourite columnist at the paper seeking advice on getting into the business. He told me exactly what I hoped he wouldn't tell me: that I should go back to school and study journalism. So, after a four-year English primer, I headed south to the University of Regina's journalism school for my finish coat. After the first term, I got an internship at – of all places – the StarPhoenix, the paper I grew up reading.

Where do columnists come from?

It was a freezing January day when the paper's new barn kitten reported for duty, greeted loudly by the larger-than-life Assistant City Editor Doug McConachie. I was sent to a restaurant that had been ransacked the night before. The photographer told me what questions to ask the owner, and I was nothing but grateful. His photo went on A1. My story went on A8 with no byline. Not a touchdown but at least I didn't fumble.

Later that week, I wrote about a time capsule in the ancient downtown arena that was going to be demolished, cramming info from six interviews into about 375 words. What a keener. On Saturday, I hit the front page with a sizzling exposé of a little old lady who got her mobility scooter fixed for free at the local garage. (Clearly, planes didn't crash every day in Saskatoon.)

As a kid, I used to sit on the front step and read the paper in the warm spring sunshine. I remember the smell more than the stories – the scent of warm newsprint, like a freshly ironed shirt. I was most interested in the columnists. What a great job that would be, to use a pen to skewer the high and mighty and make real people laugh. And how completely unattainable.

There were no columnist schools that I knew of. How the heck did somebody become one?

But my internship meant I was getting there. By the end of my first week as a baby reporter, I was pulling papers out of a cryogenically cold mailbox and finding my own stories in them. Ice-cold newsprint smelled pretty great, too.

To my delight, McConachie got the go-ahead to hire me full-time after I finished school. He was a great boss, an old-school go-getter and hyper-extrovert who always had your back and saved his most creative writing for expense forms. Sadly, cancer got him at 65 not long after he retired. I owe him a lot.

My first beat was "cops and courts," hanging out at a provincial court, keeping an eye on first appearances to see if anything interesting came up. I could well have been the strangest crime reporter the paper ever had. I was always more interested in the quirky stories than the blood and guts. When the city's landmark double-decker ice cream bus had its windows smashed, I was all over it. The accused had romantic designs on one of the employees and I fashioned some cockamamie yarn about broken glass, broken hearts and ice cream.

Then one day, Joyce Milgaard flagged me down in court. She was working to exonerate her son David, the convicted killer. I'd interviewed her on the phone for a few stories. Her son's claims of innocence were being disputed vigorously by retired cops and the original prosecutor. I was giving her the benefit of the doubt at that point. She said she had a lead on the possible real killer and wanted my help knocking on some doors in his old neighbourhood. She swore me to secrecy and I complied because I wanted to stay on her good side in case she was right. She was, of course, and finally got her son out of prison after a 22-year travesty of justice.

After a year on the court beat, I had a decision to make. There was an unexpected opening in the entertainment department to replace the theatre writer. It was a chance to take advantage of some of the drama classes I'd taken for my English degree. Tempting. On the other hand, I'd be turning in my real-reporter badge. But the crime scene was already wearing me down – the apartment fire where kids were killed, the monster who cut the head off a puppy in front of his kids. I made the move, agonizing about what McConachie would think. He let me go with no hard feelings.

My new beat was one of those jobs that doesn't seem like a job – reviewing movies, concerts and plays, covering arts news. On good days, I couldn't believe it either. It was so cool, I felt guilty. I vowed never to take it for granted, and I never have. And then one day, it got even better. My new editor, Pat Macsymic, paused by my desk and said, "How would you like to write a column?" Are you kidding me? I restrained the urge to jump up and down and gleefully set about the task.[1]

I had to keep doing everything else on the beat, but that was that. Nobody told me what the column was supposed to be about. No one, ever, told me what I should write about. And no one ever told me to stop doing it. So I didn't. But the funny thing is, I *still* don't know where columnists come from.

This book is part memoir and part anthology. I've interviewed hundreds of musicians in my career, from B.B. King to Gene Simmons. It has always amazed me how a hit song endures, whether it's about love, heartbreak or highways to hell. How different from a columnist's little ditties, which are here one minute and gone the next. Even the good ones!

I view this book as a way to change that one tiny bit – a chance to reintroduce my best columns and describe where I was in my life at the time. The songs and the stories behind them, in a way. I hope you like them. They go something like this . . .

---

1   What the heck? A footnote? My first column ran on December 18, 1991. It was about video stores.

Chapter 1

Work: Nobody Said It Would Be Hard

Wait a second, you got here awfully fast. I hate to ask, but did you read the introduction yet? I've been known to skip them myself, if that makes you feel any better. In the unlikely event that you, let's say, forgot, I'll just wait here for a few minutes while you catch up.

Hey! Welcome back! Let's get going.

I thought I'd start with the place I've spent most of my adult life. It's the newsroom of the StarPhoenix, a daily newspaper in Saskatoon, Saskatchewan.

This is where I've written almost every column I've ever done. Writing a column in a newsroom is like trying to play chess in a chicken coop. Distractions abound. It's a large, open room with the desks side-by-side and no real workspace dividers. It could easily be converted into a factory for sewing counterfeit Levis, something a few newspaper owners might actually have considered over the years.

But it's not a textile factory, so maybe it's a text factory – for the manufacture and repair of democracy. This is where reporters spin their yarns.

In countless movies and TV shows, no workplace is so carefully *unglam-ourized* as the newsroom. All you see are messy desks and sweaty reporters yelling into phones. The editor, kept in a glass cube like an important bug, is always lecturing a cub reporter.

"Parker! If you don't get me that picture before deadline, you're finished!"

And it's all true! The desks are messy. The reporters are animated. Copy editors delete all your excellent exclamation marks. And the boss always wants the Spiderman exclusive.

I'm awed by newspaper reporters, how hard they work to get a story, how much they care. They're friendly, outgoing and down-to-earth. Their attire is alarmingly casual. I had a colleague who wore a blue jean shirt every day for 11 years – hedging his bet on the Levis factory, maybe.

Reporters are curious. They are purebred underdogs who devour gossip. They're not the least bit self-conscious. When my niece was in Grade 9, I took her to the office for a day. Her first and lasting impression of profes-sional journalists?

"They sure swear a lot."

Reporters don't make a lot of money and a lot of good ones quit to get better paying jobs in important government offices and key industries – places where adults wear Proper Business Attire. Are there any hard feelings or petty jealousies when honest reporters sell their souls to Crown corpora-tions and double their incomes? Gosh, no, none at all. We just say that they went over to the "Dark Side."

The ones who stay have a sense of mission and lofty ideals. They are determined to hold powerful people accountable, to fight for democracy, to save the world. They love their jobs. That's why they stay put. Or maybe they just hate the idea of wearing shoes that lace up. But it's all very professional, very laudable. Which brings me to . . .

The day I slimed the mayor

So there's me in the middle of all this journalistic virtue, plying my trade in the Department of Entertainment. Rarely do I cross paths with powerful politicians or titans of industry. Maybe that's a good thing. Years after the day I hosted my niece, when it was time for me to host my own Grade 9 sons for Take Our Kids to Work Day, things did not go as planned.

The night before, I was in the garage fooling around with some gunpowder from fireworks. (What? Doesn't everybody experiment with explosives in their free time?) In the interest of science, I wanted to see if the black powder I had extracted from a dismantled cherry bomb was just some sort of packing or actually flammable. The best way to find out was to see if it burned. I held a lighter to a small pile of it in an ashtray. Nothing happened. I held it awhile longer. No results. Just as I was about to give up, a three-foot plume of flame flashed around my right hand.

The voice inside my head, the one that had told me a few minutes earlier that this would be a cool experiment, was now apologizing profusely. I retreated to the house in a significant amount of pain and discreetly kept my hand immersed in a salad bowl full of ice cubes for the remainder of the evening.

By morning, most of my palm was covered in a plump, tender, juicy blister. I was actually relieved. With no open sore, I didn't need a bandage. I could therefore hide my injury.

The first event of Grade 9 Day was a press conference at the Canadian Legion to publicize a war documentary produced by local filmmaker Tony Towstego. He was there to greet me. I've known Tony for years but I had forgotten about his Vise-Grip handshake. He grabbed a fistful of burn bubble and squeezed. I was suddenly aware that my palm was wet. "Oh, my God," I thought, "Tony just popped my blister." It must have oozed after he released because he didn't notice. Still, I needed to find a washroom, and fast.

At that instant, the mayor materialized. I should have known. He never missed an event.

"Oh hello, Mayor Atchison!"

The mayor thrust forth his hand. I couldn't insult him by refusing to shake. I was trapped. He grasped my mitt. His Worship didn't flinch. The lack of reaction was puzzling, like the fuse going out before the dynamite explodes. The mayor found another hand to shake, and another. Of course! The man had shaken millions of hands. Clearly, many of them had been sweaty or greasy or recently sneezed into. I can only assume that my oozing blister wasn't worth losing a vote over. Long live democracy.

That's as close as I ever got to covering city council. I was happy to stick to the entertainment beat. There are no hands to shake when you're sitting in the dark watching a play or a concert. The only downside is getting teased by civilians and colleagues.

"You get paid to go to shows? Must be nice."

It took me years to find a retort: "Well, nobody said it would be hard."

But that's not entirely true. There are perils, particularly when you write concert reviews. If you get the title of a song wrong, it just proves you don't have a clue what you're talking about. One morning after a Céline Dion concert, a woman phoned practically in tears because I wrote that the second song of the night was *The Power of Love*. It was. I took notes. She would not believe me.

"I should know. That song is very important to me," she said. If I were speaking to her in person, I would have started slowly backing out of the room.

It's an odd, disconnected vibe working at a concert when everyone else is bonding in their love for the artist – the ultimate outside-looking-in experience. It makes you feel like you've snuck into a Black Mass.

One night at a Mötley Crüe show, I found a great spot at the far back of the arena where no one would bother me. In the dark, wearing a ball cap, I was invisible. Then a group of young guys plunked themselves down in front of me. They had their own reason to be discreet. They lit up a joint and passed it back and forth.

After everyone had a drag, one of the guys turned around and handed me the joint. I took a pretend puff just to fit in and handed it back to him. Over the crushing noise of the band, he shouted something to me. I said, "What?" He said, "You reviewed Metallica, right? That was an awesome show!" So much for being invisible.

Another night in the same building, KISS paid for my supper – more or less. It started with a phone interview I did weeks before with the band's bass player, Gene Simmons. He was at his bombastic best, selling the show. "There's enough tonnage to build a fort," he expounded. "There's enough electricity to light a small city. There's enough sound system to knock five pounds off any fat girl within 1,000 yards of the stage."

The story ran a week or so before the band got to town. On the day of the show, KISS's road manager got me a backstage pass and asked if I could personally deliver four copies of the paper to the band because the guys liked to read about themselves when they were putting on their makeup. Whoa, I was about to meet KISS.

But not really. When I got there, the road manager barely remembered the request. "Thanks," he said, taking the papers. "Well, feel free to hang around." Me? The illustrious rock reviewer, reduced to a courier boy? I was hurt, I have to say. Revenge was in order.

I was left wandering around backstage with an hour to kill before show time. That's when I chanced upon the catering room for the crew. Various roadies were lined up at the buffet. I joined them. That's how I got back at Gene – by eating an excessive amount of KISS stew. Stew. Surely the least rock 'n' roll dish of all time.

I love writing columns about work. It's a chance to put the unsung heroes of my profession in the spotlight, to dispel notions that journalists are heartless muckrakers or careless with the facts. Maybe some are, but I've never worked with one. It's also a way to let the reader look backstage and, as they say, see how the sausage gets made.

For example, I was tortured on the job once. It happened at the Fringe theatre festival. I was covering a show called *Train Your Man*. A bizarre series of coincidences came together when a cellphone rang in the theatre and the performer ordered me to join her on stage. She made me kneel down, kiss the floor and do an embarrassing dance. And she was just getting started, unfortunately.

I eventually got a column out of it, so the torture was almost worth it. And I found out later there was one more plot twist for me. Read on.

A phone rang in the theatre

Thursday, Aug. 3, 2006, 2 p.m. I conduct a pleasant phone interview with actress Shirley Kirchmann of South Africa for a story on the Fringe.

Kirchmann has a play called *Train Your Man*. She finds my first name unusual.

Friday, Aug. 4, 4:30 p.m. I head down to the Fringe to review two plays: *Audible* in Venue 3 and *Train Your Man* in Venue 5. I realize I've left my laminated media pass at home. I purchase a button for admittance and, therefore, look like any old member of the audience.

5:45 p.m. Have chat with a Fringe usher about audience participation in shows. She got picked twice in one year. I confess that my greatest Fringe fear is getting picked from the audience to go onstage. She, too, is going to *Train Your Man* that night.

7:02 p.m. *Audible* ends. I see Shirley Kirchmann outside Venue 5. Since we've never met in person, I think about going over and saying hi. But I don't.

7:20 p.m. Using the company laptop, I write the review for *Audible* and send it in using the office cellphone. I don't use this phone for regular calling. In fact, I've never even heard it ring.

9:03 p.m. *Train Your Man* begins.

Kirchmann depicts several women betrayed by their mates and proposes they be trained like dogs using the Barbara Woodhouse method. Kirchmann needs "volunteers" from the audience. She points her riding crop and says, "You, you and you." Three males sheepishly go up front. None of them is me, thank God. Kirchmann orders them to kneel, takes an ink stamp, and stamps TRAINED on their foreheads in inch-high letters. Then she feeds them Milk Bone dog biscuits and dismisses them. The audience is loving it.

9:11 p.m. Brrringg! Brrringg! An audience member's cellphone rings. It's one of those horrible, shrill, metallic ringtones that sound like old-fashioned dial phones from the 1940s. And it's coming from my corner of the theatre.

I'm disgusted. How rude. Cellphones going off in plays and movies drive me nuts. I'm the first to sigh, shake my head and glare at these idiots when their phones ring. But wait! I've got a cellphone with me! Oh. My. God. I reach down and pull out my phone.

9:12 p.m. "Come here," Kirchmann commands me. I'm as angry as she is. How could I be so stupid? I tell her "Just a minute," and trot toward the door. She thinks I'm running away and she swats my behind with her crop. I open the theatre door and toss my phone into a conveniently located garbage receptacle.

9:12 p.m. and 30 seconds. "Sit on your knees," Kirchmann orders. I don't know what this means, but I kneel down.

"Kiss the stage," she says. I bend over and kiss the floor. The audience laughs at the cellphone idiot. "What are you going to do the next time you come to a play?" she asks.

"I'm going to throw my phone in the garbage," I promise.

"Good," she says.

My backside still stinging, I'm sent back to my seat. Phew.

9:13–9:40 p.m. The show progresses. Kirchmann, who's wonderfully funny and certifiably insane, portrays an obnoxious boy who's rude to his mother and a loutish man who's rude to his wife. Clearly, men must learn how to treat women. I'm trying to concentrate, but I'm wondering how I'm going to get my phone back.

9:40 p.m. Volunteers are needed for the next scene. Kirchmann chooses an older man and, yes, me. She teaches us four dance moves involving footwork, jumping and pelvic rotations. This morphs into a break-up dance-of-rage, and we discover we are enacting a wronged woman stomping on her ex's car, wiping her behind with his MasterCard and peeing on his pillow.

We kneel down. Kirchmann stamps TRAINED on the older man and gives him a Milk Bone. Then she gives me a Milk Bone and stamps TRAINED on my forehead and both sides of my face. Then she gets me to lift my shirt and stamps TRAINED seven times on my stomach.

9:43 p.m. The older man is set free. I am not.

"Get me that green shirt," Kirchmann says. It's a small tank top with an unprintable sexual command printed on it. "Kneel down," she says, putting the shirt on.

9:43 p.m. and 27 seconds. "What's your name?" Kirchmann asks. "Cam," I say.

There's a pause as it sinks in. "Oh. Shit," Kirchmann says.

The audience erupts. Even I manage to laugh. Kirchmann shakes her head and explains to those who didn't already know that the person she's putting the blocks to is the one who is reviewing her show. More general hilarity.

9:44 p.m. The segment already started, Kirchmann has no choice but to continue. The scene can't be described in detail, although I'm supposed to give an animal cracker a compliment and then lick it sensuously. I panic instead and gobble it down. Calmly, Kirchmann hands me another and I finally lick it. The audience claps. I take my seat.

10:02 p.m. The show ends. Fringe volunteer Calvin brings me my phone. Kirchmann comes out and apologizes. Not necessary, I tell her. She did exactly what the situation called for. And besides, I deserved it. Me, of all people, a cellphone idiot!

10:31 p.m. Safe and sound back home, I get my wife to dial the cellphone. It goes off. It has a musical ring tone. She checks the phone's call history. It hasn't received a call since the day before.

10:32 p.m. The truth comes too late to set me free. A phone rang in the theatre that night. But not mine.

August 12, 2006

Knocking columns together is all in a day's work

With a strain and a slap and a lusty cry, another columnist has entered the world.

It brings a tear to my eye. No, wait, that's sawdust. Anyway, this is no ordinary columnist. This is Mike Holmes, home repair demigod, TV star, super hunk and personal saviour of overalls everywhere, by gosh.

Welcome to the wordsmithing trade, Mike. Since you're the new guy, a little orientation is in order. Take this box here and fill it with commas. Just kidding! We do that to all the rookies. That's actually the semicolon box. By the time you're a journeyman newspaper writer, you'll know the difference between commas and semicolons. (Actually, you probably won't.)

I see you've already finished your first column, Mike. You're writing about the work you did in New Orleans building a house to replace one that was destroyed by Hurricane Katrina. Looks fairly plumb. Lots of sturdy adjectives propping up the sentences. Nice use of the dash – not everyone can do that. A couple of your paragraphs are too long but we've got editors here who can trim those. Editors are our building inspectors. They can make your life extremely difficult if they don't like you. Luckily, they happen to love Scotch. This is a hint.

As an apprentice writer, you're probably wondering what tools and equipment you will need. You know those heavy canvas pants with side pockets and hammer loops? Well, don't buy those. The truth is, columnists wouldn't wear pants at all if they could get away with it. They compromise by wearing Dockers. Get lots of those. Try to find some with reinforced seats. More than anything else, the job of column writing entails a lot of heavy sitting. For the same reason, you won't need boots. If you're a good columnist, you will be going out of your way to step on a few toes, but you'll be perfectly safe in flip-flops or something with Velcro straps.

Your tool box should contain a dictionary (new, never opened), a pencil (similar to a carpenter's pencil but round), prescription eyeglasses (computer monitors are hell on the eyes) and a Milwaukee 12-inch dual-bevel sliding compound mitre saw with digital angle readout and dual integrated work lights. You won't need it, but it's damn cool.

Okay, so you've arrived at the job site (or "office"). Time to get to work. No, Mike! Not the sledgehammer! I know your cubicle is small but you can't just. . . . Hey, that's pretty nice. Really opened the place up. Your guys did a great job rerouting the ductwork, too; I never would have thought of using five-inch. The only problem I see is an awkward transition between your doorway and . . .

Coffee, Mike? I know you prefer Nescafé. You might notice that columnists don't take coffee breaks, per se. Instead, they dedicate themselves to drinking coffee from nine to five and throw in the odd writing break every couple of hours. To the layperson, it might look like they're loafing. Not so. They're procrastinating. Measure twice and cut once. That's how we do it around here.

Eventually, the deadline will start to loom. I'm going to level with you, Mike; you're going to need a column idea, and soon. Columnists hate coming up with column ideas as much as you hate shoddy workmanship. Don't deny it. I've seen your angry look – your chiselled jaw, those blue eyes squinting, biceps bulging over rippling pecs. Oh my, where was I? Right, column ideas.

Here's a tip: check today's paper. Find something you can get outraged about. Outrage is absolutely necessary. It's the lumber of the column-writing profession. But don't worry. It's just a matter of picking over a pile of headlines and finding something without getting too many slivers. Hey, here's a good one: "Military judge overrules firing of Khadr's lawyer."

"WHAT?" says the columnist, doing a spit-take with a mouthful of Nescafé. "THAT'S OUTRAGEOUS! I CAN'T BELIEVE IT! WHERE'S MY KEYBOARD?"

That's the spirit. You've got your blood up. You could cut through high-voltage wires with your Sawzall and not even notice. But wait a second there, Sparky. Now, you've got to do some research. Research in column writing is like sanding drywall. No one actually likes doing it, but it's going to look pretty rough if you don't. Okay, so you're going to have to find out who this Khadr guy is and why he needed a lawyer and why the lawyer was fired and . . . and . . . Mike, your eyes are glazing over. You're thinking about grout, aren't you?

Okay, forget the Khadr idea. I'll write about rude people talking in movie theatres and you can do something on geothermal heating. The main thing is that we're colleagues. I have to admit, I've always been intimidated by your high standards compared to my own home handyman repairs. But now we're finally on an equal footing. Get it? Equal footing? Put down the router, Mike. I'll shut up now.

April 11, 2009

Really, people? That's all it takes?

I went to a concert the other night and a hockey game broke out. No, that's not it. I went to an arena the other night and a concert broke out. That's what happened. But there's more. A lot of excitement broke out as well. It happens at every concert. People get excited at concerts. You take this for granted. I happen to be a paid observer of people being excited. One thing I've noticed in my job is that people get excited about things that aren't necessarily that exciting. Like, for instance, "Hello, Saskatoon."

Musician: HELLO, SASKATOON!

Audience: WOO HOO!

Really, people?

Go to any concert and at some point you can count on one of the musicians saying the name of your city. (Unless that musician is Bob Dylan. You can't count on Bob Dylan to say much of anything, not even the words to his own songs.)

But musicians who want to whip up excitement need only remember where they happen to be at that moment. A struggle for some, no doubt, but not all.

I professionally observed quite a lot of excitement at a recent Brad Paisley concert. One of the show openers was Dierks Bentley. The likable Arizonan started his high-energy set wearing a plain, ordinary plaid shirt. It gave him a workingman look, like he might just throw his microphone down in the middle of a song and start loading a truck.

Dierks sang and jogged around the stage, he bent over and slapped palms with people up front and went through half a dozen of his songs. Then there was a short break. Dierks ran backstage for a few seconds. When he re-emerged, people clapped. Fair enough – you welcome him back; it's only polite. But this wasn't just a "Hey, you left and came back" clap. It was an excited "Woo hoo!" kind of clap. The reason? Dierks was now wearing a T-shirt.

Really, people?

One can only imagine the ecstasy that would have been unleashed if Dierks Bentley had removed his plaid shirt on stage. But this was a country music show and that's more of a rock show thing to do. In front of a crowd of 5,000, the removal of a shirt by a rock star gets the following response: WOO HOO!

Concerts are a leading cause of overexcitement. But they're not the sole cause. People also get overexcited about New Year's Eve, getting their faces on a stadium's big screen, and summer movie blockbusters. People also tend to get overexcited about dessert. Have you noticed this? You'll eat a fantastic meal, for which one of God's creatures gave its life, and it's "Oh, that was pretty good." Then the server will come around with a dessert menu and you turn into a nervous, giggling ninny. "Chocolate mocha peanut butter pecan mudslide pie? Oh, why not, tee-hee-hee."

But concerts take the cake. I've seen singers get applause for doing nothing more than sitting down. Midpoint in a concert, they often like to "slow things down a little bit." The band goes backstage and the headliner straps on an acoustic guitar (woo hoo!) and sits on a stool that a roadie has just set down for him (woo hoo!). Then he'll take a sip from a bottle of water (woo hoo!). He'll mop some sweat with a towel (woo hoo!). He'll check to see if the guitar is in tune (woo hoo!). Imagine going through life with all this affirmation. Your toast pops – brilliant! You put on your socks – brilliant! You spit out your toothpaste – brilliant! Is it any wonder superstars get loopy?

A concert audience pretty much comes pre-excited for the star's convenience. You can imagine the ecstasy that ensues when someone does a drum solo. Oh dear, the drum solo. Everyone claims to love the drum solo, yet has anyone ever heard one that was too short? It starts with a beat, which is good, but then spirals into random bashing. The power! The energy! The tedium! I feel the same way about drum solos that I do about trains. Things are going along just fine until one crosses your path. Then all you can do is sit and wait until it's over.

Still, the biggest reactions in concerts come when the star says something that seems to break down the barrier between celebrity and fan, that tells the ordinary people in the bleachers that their music idol understands them, respects them and, perhaps, even loves them.

HOW YA DOIN', SASKATOON?

WOO HOO!

Aforementioned West Virginia country star Brad Paisley is a master at it. He says hi to "God's Frozen People." He plays a few electric guitar notes of *O Canada*. People eat it up. Whenever he sings his song *Alcohol,* the big screen shows pictures of well-known bars, taverns and pubs in the city he's in.

Rodeo's: Woo hoo! O'Shea's: Woo hoo! The Deuce: Woo hoo!

Really, people? It's not as if Brad Paisley was out all day shivering, taking video.

But the thing that gets an even bigger response, the thing that Brad Paisley uses to take an already whipped-up crowd and turn it into latté foam, is a magic spell that consists of seven magic words:

"The band got their Tim Hortons today."

The audience erupts. Really, people?

February 28, 2009

How to cover the country without leaving home

The Canadian Country Music Association (CCMA) awards were allegedly held in Saskatoon last weekend. I say "allegedly" because, although I was there, I wasn't there.

It's a strange feeling to cover an event that you're not really at. You feel a bit like a phantom. (Hmm, Phantom of the Rodeo – sounds like a country and western band.)

I swear I didn't cover the show and I have pictures to prove it. It's all because of a bunker called the Media Room. The Media Room boasts white cinderblock walls, rubber baseboards, tile floors, fluorescent lighting and folding chairs. If you had to get mug shots of suspects and interrogate them, you'd do it here. In fact, that's exactly what the room is for.

The Media Room is where the CCMA publicists put the media. Small TV monitors broadcast the actual show, but it might as well come from Vladivostok. All you get of the real show is the echoing booms of live music upstairs. Essentially, you're taking refuge in a country music bomb shelter.

"Hey kids, don't waste those Dean Brody CDs, we only have enough for six months."

Awards show organizers have very strict rules to control the Media Room. Due to "extremely limited space," only one writer and one photographer from the StarPhoenix were allowed in.

The rules were slightly different for the host broadcaster, CBC. There were CBC people everywhere. CBC national people. CBC regional people. CBC local people. CBC producers, CBC publicists, CBC executives, CBC publicity executives, CBC executive publicists, CBC camera people, CBC reporters in both official languages. Someone opened the door on me when I was in the bathroom – a CBC bathroom door lock checker, I can only assume.

A blue dot on my media pass said I was allowed to be in the Media Room and nowhere else. I took a stroll down the hallway. Michelle Wright swished by in a flowing silver gown. She looked like fireworks.

A stagehand was guarding an empty room: the room where Taylor Swift's family would wait until they were escorted to their seats. OMG! OMG!

OMG! I had to see it. There was a leather chaise and a flower in a vase. And beef jerky. Beef jerky!

Before the Tasers came out, I scurried back to the Media Room. Someone had promised us water, but none was coming.

We had to be in the Media Room by 2 p.m. The show didn't start until five. That's a lot of time to wonder if Taylor Swift's family was going to finish all the beef jerky.

My stomach growled. I talked to Sam Chow, the CCMA auditor who had flown in from Toronto the night before with the winners' names in gold envelopes.

"Did you lock them in your briefcase overnight?" I asked.

"No," Sam Chow said.

At 4:15 p.m., a chef came in and set up the Media Room buffet. Well, I never. If the CCMAs thought they could distract us with – hey, free beer! Oh, and barbecued chicken. And hot spinach dip. And beef tenderloin au jus. Okay, well, maybe the Media Room wasn't such a bad place to be after all.

My colleagues hit the buffet like bums on a bologna sandwich. I tried to grab a dinner roll without getting my hand gnawed off. Then, suddenly, it was 5 p.m. and time to start covering the show we weren't covering.

Carolyn Dawn Johnson got her trophy upstairs. She gave a speech saying she felt great. Then she came down to the Media Room for interrogation. The media asked her how she felt. She felt great.

And so it went. Dean Brody won. He felt great. Jason Blaine, too. And Johnny Reid. All the winners felt great. And they were all so nice!

The evening flashed by like fireworks. The highlight was Taylor Swift. The CCMA invented a new award just for her called the "Generation" Award. I think it was mainly about generating ratings for CBC.

At 6:30 p.m. or so, a hush descended on the Media Room. Because they took the tenderloin away? No. Because Taylor Swift had agreed to come down. Grown men and women of the media were trying to look cool. But what they were thinking was OMG! OMG! OMG!

Taylor Swift came in, a placid vision of confidence and grace. She posed for pictures. Someone asked her how she felt. She felt great.

And then, like a vision, Taylor Swift was gone. She was so nice! Her publicist came back a minute later and said that Taylor Swift was impressed with how friendly the media were. "We were going to throw buns, but they took them away," I said.

Lessons learned: Country musicians are so nice! Buffets are never wrong. And the more award shows you cover, the fewer you see.

September 16, 2012

Work-a-day world isn't kids' stuff

Nothing triggers lingering self-doubt like Take Our Kids to Work Day.

The annual event, perpetrated upon Grade 9 students across North America, has a noble goal: to get kids thinking about careers early on in their high school education. The choices are endless.

1. **Forklift Operator**
   Pros: Driving is fun.
   Cons: Is that a foreman-shaped lump under that pile of pallets?

2. **Police Officer**
   Pros: Guns! Cool!
   Cons: Yikes! Guns!

3. **Firefighter**
   Pros: Trucks! Cool!
   Cons: Wet Dalmatian kisses! Yuck!

As a side effect, Wake Your Surly Teenager Up Early Day also gets adults thinking. Thinking things like, "Oh God, what have I done with my sorry excuse for a life?" Let's face it: most jobs aren't that rewarding. The expression "another day, another dollar" isn't an exaggeration, it's an audited financial statement.

It's one thing to trudge to work every day, do your job, and trudge home. It's quite another to have an innocent bystander witness what could very well be a very sucky job. It upsets the natural order of things, disturbs the routine. And routine must not be tampered with. It's routine that gets you through your working life. Have you ever heard a retirement speech? They're all the same. "I can't believe how fast the last 30 (35, 40, 60) years have gone by, blah, blah, blah."

Forty-five years don't just disappear on their own, you know. The secret is routine. Used properly, routine develops a healthy, mind-numbing effect, like a liberal dose of Novocain injected directly under the gum line of your ambition, so you don't feel the screeching drill of harsh reality churning its way into the nerve endings of your broken dreams. (Guess who had a dental appointment this week?) The point is, before you know it, it's time to rinse, spit and pick up your gold watch.

Where were we? Oh yes, Expose Your Most Vulnerable Parts Day. We had a bunch of kids here at the old StarPhoenix this week, exploring the many career opportunities in the fast-paced world of daily newspapering. After they were done washing my car, they got to tour the printing press. That's where the real action is: a blur of newsprint spinning from massive spools, churning out 70,000 copies an hour. The press guys were printing the *TV Times*. Copy after copy of Shania Twain's smiling, back-from-retirement-just-when-you'd-hoped-she-was-gone-forever face whirring by at the speed of light. It was so inspiring, I had to put my head between my knees until the room stopped spinning.

It was hard to tell what the Grade 9s thought about this mighty machine. It's hard to tell what Grade 9s think about anything. I haven't had time to look this up, but I'm guessing that the world poker champion is a kid in Grade 9. Are they bored? Amazed? Secretly hostile? Who knows? It's like the old joke: "How can you tell a politician is lying? His lips are moving." Instead, it's: "How can you make a Grade 9 stop listening to you? Move your lips."

We showed them the darkroom. No reaction. We showed them our mini TV studio where we do segments for the Global TV mother ship. I think one of them said "Hmm," but it might have been my stomach rumbling. We took them to an actual news conference at the police station. Their true feelings remained at large.

I'd forgotten what an awkward age Grade 9 can be. The peer pressure is enormous. You'd rather die than stand out from the crowd. You're not quite a child but not quite an adult. In other words, you're at the exact same level of maturity as one member of the StarPhoenix newsroom: the entertainment writer.

My back was up against the wall. I had no choice but to open up and show the kids what my "job" is really like. There was a murmur of approval when I told the kids we'd be seeing a movie over the lunch hour. In Grade 9 terms, that's a reaction equivalent to a street riot. We screened a subtitled German film at the Broadway Theatre about an unhappy chef and an orphan. I was impressed with the kids: they all said they enjoyed it. In fact, the only complaint was that Chad was playing his Discman too loudly.

After that, we came back to the office and looked through a pile of old movie press kits. This triggered an actual outburst of enthusiasm, not to mention a tidal wave of indignation when I said something unflattering about Adam Sandler. By then, it was time to open my mail: a box of new CDs from Universal Music.

Thus ended another exhausting day of thankless toil in the Department of Entertainment. I hope the kids learned that working for a living is serious business, and that they should stay in school and say no to drugs and all that good stuff. I also hope none of them wants my job or got a chance to tamper with the brakes on my car.

November 9, 2002

The peril of reporting in the Age of Outrage

I admit that half the entertainment value in reading the news online is found in the comments that run after a story.

There's a perverse pleasure in seeing people lose their minds, particularly over things that don't matter. For instance, the New York Times ran a recipe for Texas chili awhile back. One reader was outraged that there were beans in it.

This devolved into how Yankees don't understand the South, and suddenly they were back to fighting the Civil War. Over chili.

What's less amusing, in the Age of Outrage, are complaints about why a story exists in the first place or the motives of the media outlet dispersing it.

Here's an article the StarPhoenix posted on Facebook this week: "Canadian doctors' group warns about the adverse effects of medicinal marijuana."

The Canadian Press was reporting on an advisory by the Alberta College of Family Physicians. There was a lack of research on medical marijuana, the association said. In fact, there was more evidence of it causing "adverse events" than there was of it helping.

The story quoted the physician behind the advisory, in addition to representatives of Health Canada and the head of the Canadian Medical Cannabis Council.

I doubt the StarPhoenix posted the story because it thought the Alberta doctors were right. But the article was timely, thanks to all the interest in medical marijuana, the growing economic clout of producers and the impending legalization of stinky weed on July 1.

People read it and some objected, which is fine. But I was shocked and saddened by what they were objecting to.

"The writer who wrote this should be ashamed," commented one reader. "These doctors should be ashamed. And the Star Phoenix should be ashamed of publishing this uncritically."

A line is being crossed, and the more you look on social media, the more you see it. It's a kill-the-messenger mentality.

"The writer should be ashamed"? What are you talking about? It's news. A reporter reported about a report. That's what they do. Another comment: "What is shameful is that this fear-mongering is perpetuated in print by the Star Phoenix and any other 'news' source as being factual."

News has never been more pervasive or, I would argue, misunderstood. Some people don't know the difference between a straight news story, a column, an editorial or an advertisement. In fact, I wrote a column recently on my antipathy toward the band the Eagles and someone objected to my "review."

Sometimes it's our fault for not labelling these things properly, but seriously, how obvious do you have to be? What sustains the Age of Outrage? A theory: people are most comfortable reading things they agree with, like the opinions of like-minded, hand-picked and curated "friends" on social media. Whatever muscle people used to have for reading things that challenged their world view has atrophied.

Dovetailing perfectly is the ease with which they can respond, angrily, without a filter or second thought. In that cloud of outrage, they want the source of the opposing view extinguished, whether it's the person quoted in the story, the person who wrote it or the outlet that has distributed it. Hence the ultimate insult: calling the StarPhoenix a "news" source in quotations. How Trump-esque.

Oh, but there are far worse comments than that. It's interesting to me that you can't take a pop can back for recycling without seeing a sign that says "verbal abuse will not be tolerated." Not so in my esteemed profession. It's more like, "verbal abuse assumed and encouraged."

The mindset of "I respect your opinion but I disagree" is now apparently as old-fashioned as the Queensberry Rules of Boxing.

To summarize: a news story isn't an opinion, an opinion isn't a news story and what you just read was a column.

Now, can we get back to arguing about chili?

December 16, 2017

You gotta llove these llama ppeople

It started like any other day at the office. I scanned the headlines in the daily paper, put my feet up and sat back to read my mail. That's when I saw the shoebox. In my line of business, a shoebox on your desk in the morning is never good news.

"Sue," I called out to the receptionist, "hold all my calls and lock the doors."

"No," she shot back. I sensed some reluctance on her part, but I had more pressing matters at hand.

It was a white shoebox from Burton's shoe store, size 6 B. Price: $16.95. I lifted it carefully. It felt legit. I was starting to feel like a heel for being suspicious. I took a long swig of coffee and removed the lid with a practised hand; all those years of buying shoes finally paid off.

Inside the box was a bag. The label said "Llamaberries." It was one full kilogram of 100 per cent llama manure. The price was strategically not removed: $3.50. Beside the dung was a ransom-type note on bond paper. Plain bond paper. It went something like this: "Dear CAM FullER I JUST saw your article on Page D5 OF THE WeEkEnD ExtrA! I THOUhgt I would DroP You a . . ." The note stopped abruptly at the bottom of the first page. But I noticed that it continued on the next. I read the pages, in order, to get the full gist of the message.

A minute later, I had a llama-sized lump in my throat. I realized I was holding in my hands the very thing a hard-boiled journalist is afraid of: a response from a reader. You see, I'd cracked wise in my Exhibition column a week earlier on the topic of llamas. Mentioned the superfluous "l" in their name. Found it amusing. Llittle did I know how seriously the Llama Ppeople take that apparently innocuous second "l."

The note explained the differences between lamas and llamas and, curiously, alpacas. A Ziploc bag of alpaca fibre was included. It felt good against my hard-boiled skin. The note ended with what I could only interpret as an invitation: "sEE us AT The SHoW!"

Then the faxes started coming in. From Connie Geller of Windfield Llamas, from Cathy Merkley, alpaca breeder, from Boyd and Pat Bell of Integrity Llama Farms. Their hoof-writing varied, but the message was the same. "Come meet a llama firsthand," they urged.

"They seem harmless enough," I mused. "Maybe alpaca lunch and stop by."

I set out for the Wheatland B building on the Exhibition grounds, the agriculture side of the fair that a city slicker hardly gives a second thought. I was nervous. The wood chips under my Gucci loafers felt foreign. But I pressed on. I simply had to get the story.

Loyd Robertson would have been proud of me. I found Wheatie B without incident. It was quiet inside. Almost too quiet. The air was fresh. Almost too fresh. And then I saw them: tall, long-necked creatures with dark eyes and perfect posture. No doubt about it: those were the farmhands. As they tidied the stables, I eyeballed the livestock behind them. They were cute. They were friendly. Was there more to these modified ruminants than meets the eye?

I introduced myself to Sharon Isayew of White Star Llama Farm. "We caught the llama bug," she confessed.

Spend half an hour talking to Sharon and she'll convince you that llamas are the perfect animal. They're gentle. They hum to their babies. They're smart. They can be used to protect sheep and cattle from predators. They don't eat much or use much water. They're so clean, people transport them in the backs of their vans and motorhomes, or the front seat of their pickups. Their bathroom manners are impeccable: they share the same dung pile, making pasture cleanup a breeze. "Lots of times you'll see five or six of them all lined up."

White Star is north of Prince Albert on the Number 2 Highway. Herds of people stop in: 1,600 last year. Employee Danica Monkman handles lots of the tours. The llamas love her. She carries alfalfa pellets in her pocket.

"They're like a big cat," she said. Big, valuable cats. Sharon's son Kevin just sold a llama for $30,000. He and his sister Leanna paid their way through university with llama money. I'd already decided I like llamas. Now I was starting to respect them.

Did I mention they're good kissers? "There's nothing like a llama kiss," said Sharon. I decided to take her word for it.

Is there anything a llama can't do? Can't cure disease, can they? Almost. Boyd and Pat Bell trained a llama to behave inside their house so they could take him to seniors' homes. They visited the bedside of one crusty old fellow who never showed emotion. He reached out and petted it.

"His eyes opened, and he smiled," said Pat. "The nurse had tears in her eyes."

"We get goosebumps talking about it," Boyd added.

By the time I'd left the Llama Ppeople, I'd learned about Peruvians and Bolivian whites, about kinky and dense fibre and heat-related infertility. It was a lot to digest, especially for a biped with only one stomach. But there was one question that went unanswered: What is the extra "l" in llama for? I'm only guessing, but I think it stands for love.

July 12, 1997

Fast food poets full of inspiration

Occasionally, various writers in the StarPhoenix newsroom put everything into five syllables. Then seven. Then five again.

> **They would be bitten**
> **The haiku bug makes poets**
> **Where none existed**

The cause of all this syllabication could be traced to a haiku contest launched by Burger King to promote its new Steakhouse Burger. If only there were a press release in my email to explain this better. Oh, wait, here it is.

"You don't have to be a poet, you just have to love flame-broiled meat," said Cameron Loopstra, marketing manager of Burger King Restaurants of Canada Inc. Slow down there, cowboy. You had me at "meat."

To get the burger rolling, the company enlisted former professional wrestler Trish Stratus to launch the website MeatHaiku.com with her own composition:

> **Do yoga, eat meat**
> **Stratusfaction guaranteed**
> **Do the body good**

Wow. And I thought she was just a jock. Normally, such an email would be flipped into the trash long before it reached an internal temperature of 180 degrees Celsius. I was on the brink of doing just that when a cheesy idea presented itself.

> **Might make a column**
> **If the others can be bribed**
> **With warm meat on bread**

Here was the plan: go out and collect a selection of hamburgers from various fast-food places, then invite the hungry wits of the newsroom to a free lunch and trick them into writing my column for me. It would be like the Algonquin Round Table, but with sesame seed buns.

When I got out into fast-food-land, I noticed the new trend in marketing: make you think "steak" while you're eating a burger. Hence all the steakhouse, sirloin and Angus beef references. If only haiku could explain this better . . .

> **Patty, chopped and formed**
> **Just can't go back and pretend**
> **It's steak anymore**

The feast: Big Mac, Angus Burger and the iconic plain Hamburger from McDonald's; the new Uncle Burger and the old reliable Mama Burger from A&W; and, from Burger King, the Steakhouse Burger and the Veggie Burger.

I've got to admit, the hardest part of this stunt was spending 45 minutes in the car with the heater on high and the windows rolled up trying to keep all the food warm. It started to smell exactly like the portable classroom we had to use in Grade 7. Luckily, I got back to the office before passing out. There would be plenty of time for that later. Let the hackfleisch haiku hoedown begin. Business reporter Cassandra Kyle struck first:

Delicious Mama
Pickles and mayo are good
I like the warm cheese

The heartwarming moment was lost, however, when reporter Darren Bernhardt checked in with:

Is that you Mama?
There's something strange about you
Is that cartilage?

The Burger King Steakhouse Burger attracted a lot of attention, not all of it good. It's a big, heavy thing loaded with deep-fried onions, lettuce, tomato, cheese and, believe it or not, a layer of baked potato with all the fixings. Sports reporter Cory Wolfe, who had been fighting the flu all week, stopped by long enough to offer:

Mushy potato
on top of the hamburger?
That's my stomach's job

But not that day. Bernhardt channelled his inner three-year-old for yet another nasty attack on the poor Steakhouse.

Why is it so sloppy
Doesn't look like the picture
I want a new one

Then, court reporter Lori Coolican arrived and almost ruined the whole poetry party. "Haiku are supposed to have a seasonal reference," she declared. Hmph.

To Lori I say
Don't rain on our meat parade
It's not summer now

The most modest sandwich of the bunch was, of course, McDonald's plain lil' hamburger. Still tastes great, though, the bun so sweet, the ketchup still hot from the car heater. Said Bernhardt:

> Simple hamburger
> Where is the ham, anyway?
> Are you kidding me?

The more we stuffed ourselves, the guiltier we felt. That's the thing with fast food: we love it, and then we hate it. Perhaps this was one of those seemed-like-a-good-idea-at-the-time ideas. City Editor Heather Persson captured that feeling with lyrical flourish:

> Burger dissection
> inspection bad idea
> finger stuck down throat

There was one more thing to do, of course. At least, after the afternoon nap.

> Grease on expense claim
> A&W receipt
> Accounting for taste

October 25, 2008

Chapter 2

Waving a Keyboard
at the Weather

I'm looking out the window of the family cabin on a cloudy, cool, windy fall day. The whitecaps on the lake are moving from the upper left of my view to the lower right. A diagonal march of grey. It snowed a bit last night. Not unusual for late November. Unfortunately, it's early October.

Eleven days ago, when I was here last, it was too hot to work on the roof. On my way here yesterday, I drove through a sunny patch of pavement into a black wall of cloud that threw crystallized snow against my windshield. Two days from now, it's supposed to be like summer again.

That's the insanity of prairie weather. It gives us too-long winters and too-short summers. It taunts, tortures and tantalizes. It's not a polar climate; it's a bipolar climate.

When you live under skies that fire live ammunition over your head, it's hard not to get stuck in a permanent flinch. In Saskatchewan, we're nothing if not good flinchers.

And yet, for me, it wasn't always so. Winters are an endurance test now, but, in my childhood, they were a natural wonder. I remember dumping snow out of my boots. I remember the crisp, metallic smell of a snow hut. I remember my mom taking blue jeans off the clothesline that were so stiff and frozen you could stand them up on their own. But I honestly don't remember ever feeling cold.

If winter was the season at hand, you made the most of it: tobogganing on Saturdays, shinny games on the rink after school (using textbooks for goal posts), and the Big Pile of Snow at recess. I don't really know why there was a Big Pile of Snow in the middle of the playground every winter, what it was for or where it came from, but it was a white magnet. In the break between science and spelling, the snow pile taught its own lessons. The big kids owned the top. If you ventured near the summit, they'd gently place a boot on your forehead and send you sliding back down. Smaller kids were happy just to scoop tunnels at base camp. And so it went, from the privileged few on top to the great masses below. Little did we know we were climbing a snowy sociological metaphor.

And then we get older. And the only way old people can have fun with snow is to complain about it. Writing about the weather and seasons is now my coping strategy. It's only mildly cathartic, but at least misery loves snowsuited company. Waving a keyboard at the weather won't tame it, but it's enough to keep your blood pumping.

Every prairie dweller has a weather war story: crossing a lake in a storm (done that – terrifying), collecting huge hailstones in thunder and lightning, driving through a snowstorm. Now that is scary. Driving in a snowstorm is horrible. Horrible. I remember, as a teenager in my Corolla, trying to follow my dad in his pickup on a highway near Candle Lake on a Christmas tree expedition. The day had been fine to start with. Aren't they always? But a storm blew in and there was a foot of snow on the highway in no time. I could barely see the tail lights of the truck ahead, so I had to speed up, which increased the chances of spinning out on the layer of ice under the drifts. Every instinct tells you to slow down before you hit the ditch, but you can't because you need the momentum to keep going. And, if you stop, you get hit from behind or chopped into ditch debris by the first snowplow. We made it to the cabin, somehow. That's when I noticed something was different about the front of my car. The sporty fibreglass spoiler under the front bumper was gone, sheared off by the drifts. It was a sobering sight. I knew, then, how Second World War fighter pilots felt when they landed their planes and noticed parts shot clean off.

In my columns, I've praised a few months. (June's reviews are always glowing.) And, yes, I've heaped invective on others. Take February. Please.

Why does it have only 28 days? Why does it rearrange its schedule and hang around for another 24 hours every four years? What's the point of February 2, also known as Groundhog Day? Where I live on the Prairies, the occasion lacks (to put it diplomatically) relevance. I once had a job painting a Dairy Queen sign pole on the first day of May. It was so cold out I had to wear long underwear. So if the most dire prediction that a confused, sleep-deprived groundhog can come up with is six more weeks of winter starting February 3, I'll take the deal.

But then summer comes and you forget what you were complaining about. And fall arrives and it's clenching time again. The worse it gets, the more I write. Anything to keep warm.

I'm glad you chose this chapter. Unless you're a friend of January or March, I don't think you'll be disappointed. I've included one of the most fun and frustrating columns I've ever written. It's called "Mmm . . . Smells Like Saskatoon." It's about defining a place by how it smells. I remember sitting at my desk in the newsroom, eyes closed, my face stretching into comical contortions as I willed myself to remember the scent of new-mown lawn and –40 degree air. My co-workers probably thought I was in distress. I'm just glad no one got out the portable defibrillator.

Receding snow yields riches galore

The nice thing about snow is that it covers things up. The nice thing about spring is that it melts the snow. The nice thing about melted snow is that you can find things in it. Sometimes, the things you can find are actually things you want to find, which is nice.

Money, for instance. Springtime in Saskatoon is treasure-hunting season. Every parking meter in town sprouts from a base of hidden coins. Countless shivering people wearing mittens attempted to plug their parking meters all winter long, only to watch helplessly as their loonies and quarters cascaded into the white blanket at their feet. Hence the term "snow bank."

But how to find that king's ransom? It's not unusual – unless there's curling on TV – to see elderly men with metal detectors creatively enhancing their Old Age Security by scanning the ground around parking meters. But it would take ages for a metal detector to pay for itself, especially if you include the parking tickets you'll incur when you get so excited you forget to plug your own meter.

Since the coins are going to be embedded in ice like prehistoric insects in amber, there has to be an easier, cheaper way of getting at them. May I suggest "Pick-a-Pick," a vending machine that dispenses ice picks at $1 each. Once the idea is launched on *Dragon's Den*, there will be one on every street corner.

Dragons: "Do you have any sales yet?"

You: "No, but . . ."

Dragons: "GET OUT!!!"

Okay, so maybe a bunch of people hanging around downtown with ice picks isn't such a great idea. But at least it would scare off those old guys with their metal detectors.

It's not all treasure under the snow, of course. Dog owners know this. To them, spring means plastic bags, gloves and gaggingly gross scoop duty. I tell you, it's just awful having to sip my Saturday morning coffee and look out the window at my poor wife enduring this chore.

Spring rituals vary from age to age and culture to culture. The ancients ate preserved meat to remind them of the fresh meat to come. Ham at Easter, therefore. There were songs, dances and festivals. Here in Saskatchewan, our time-honoured tradition is bottle picking. I remember doing this with my dad. He had a weakness for cheap, unrestorable old cars that made the experience even more . . . memorable. There we were, on the shoulder of some highway in a 1960s Vauxhall Envoy (a block of wood serving as the gas pedal), hunting for empty beer bottles at two miles an hour. And there were LOTS of empties, enough to fill the trunk if you found a good stretch and beat the competition. Yes, the competition. We weren't the only ones out there doing it. This was the 1970s. Pride hadn't been invented yet.

Think about this for a minute. A ditch full of empty booze bottles meant that people didn't just litter all winter long, they did an awful lot of drinking and driving as well. And to think all this occurred at night down icy highways on slippery nylon tires in cars that couldn't defrost their own windows. Sociologically speaking, it makes bullfighting look like wholesome entertainment.

Trudging toward the grocery store, on a day that was at least eight degrees below normal and spring a mere rumour, I looked up at a magnificent pile of dirt and ice in the parking lot.

Scientists should study this. They could time the melt and learn about climate change. They could sift through the remnants for priceless artifacts, all those fascinating coffee lids, bottle caps and bread tags painting a vivid picture of civilization. Such discoveries to be made! Such knowledge to be gained!

Then again, I might be making a mountain out of a mall hill.

March 26, 2011

Mmm . . . smells like Saskatoon

There is a fiscal year. There is a calendar year. Saskatoon has an olfactory year.

The city, part garden and part freezer, home to smokestacks and festivals built on wood chips, can mark the passage of time by smells as much as by seasons.

May is the beginning of the olfactory year. It's when the trees spring to life, the grass greens up and the city's people finally release themselves from a winter-long, full-body clench. It's OK; you can put down the snow scraper now.

By May, it's safe to lower one's shoulders from ear height and to breathe in the familiar but forgotten smells of a new year coming to life: the spicy scent of poplar trees waking up, the cold metallic freshness of sprinklers (tap tap tap – whirr). And, finally, the first cut of lawn, which chops the colour green into a sweet-and-sour smell. Mmm. Thank you very mulch.

Late spring and early summer are a dizzying time for smell-o-philes. Early evening is best. As the day cools, the air fills with an intoxicating mixture of blossoms: impossibly intense lilac, laundry-fresh apple and sweet plum.

Like life itself, this time of year is all the more precious for its brevity. As fast as it arrives, it will leave. You want to bottle it for later, like crab apples in jars.

It's not all airborne poetry, mind you. Aspiring north-end city councillors always pledge to fight the withering fumes of the "Wastewater" Treatment Plant. Plug your nose, but don't hold your breath. On the other end of the food cycle, there's meatpacking and oilseed crushing, not at the top of anyone's favourite smells. And don't forget the beloved river, which can positively reek fishiness.

Far from the glass-and-steel megalopolis we might like to be, Saskatoon is still a small dot on a big prairie, and there ain't a fence in the world that's going to contain the smell of fresh manure on surrounding farmland. A humbling smell, that. And if you're ever riding your bike up past Ravine Drive after spring thaw, there's an ammonia stench from a poultry operation across the river that's enough to stop you in your tracks. It's hard to feel sleek and modern when you're wearing rural perfume. But maybe the eau de toilette keeps us humble.

Summer rushes to be done, an impatient reader skipping pages. Suddenly, the wild roses are blooming. There are a bunch of them near the weir on Spadina Crescent. You smell them before you see them – sweet, unexpected wonderfulness on an early morning bike ride.

Inducted into the Summer Scents Hall of Fame are cool rain on hot pavement, wieners roasting on backyard firepits, chamomile flowers crushed under bare feet, and chlorine at the outdoor pool stirred with suntan lotion.

Exhausted from sprinting, summer rests with the earthiness of backyard produce and onion-scented compost piles. Before you know it, it's dry leaves you're smelling. Or Sunday bacon frying from a distant kitchen. Or hot leather – a football basking in the sun.

The morning air is chilly now, but scents seem to carry for miles. Emanating from north downtown are the malty-hoppy aromas of a bouncing baby batch of newborn beer from Great Western Brewing. And, from the University of Saskatchewan campus, for some strange reason, chicken soup.

Even cooler now. Wisps of snow are flying past the window. The sun can't do it alone. We need the dusty-dry smell and welcome warmth of our car heaters and home furnaces.

And finally, undeniably, freezing cold. So cold that the middle section of the newspaper remains chilled until you get to it. There's nothing like the smell of chilled newsprint in the morning. This time of year, the paper will be stuffed like a turkey with holiday flyers.

Next, unwrap the frenzy of Christmas smells, from piney tree lots to fudge in the malls to the plasticky newness of Scotch Tape.

Winter. Snow has its own smell. It's fresh, like purified water but, you know, frozen.

Cold is clean. Winter also smells like hockey tape. And bonfires beside skating rinks. And, in the coldest of the cold mornings, city bus diesel exhaust hanging in the darkness.

Snow smells when it's melting, too. In a February thaw, when hot, black shingles nibble at white drifts, it's a welcome present, a welcome pre-scent, of spring.

Our olfactory year ends in similar style, but this time the melting is for real, and the air is suddenly earthy and full of promises that may actually be kept. Then it's tar-and-gravel gumbo in the potholes, dust behind the street sweeper and the sickly sweet rot at the landfill. Time to buy a new calendar. One with blossoms on the first picture.

May 14, 2011

June joins pantheon of memorable months

Induction ceremony: The Month Hall of Fame
2010 honouree: June

Ladies and gentlemen, honoured guests, fellow months; I was truly humbled when June asked me to introduce her on this very special occasion. It's not every day of the month that a month enters the illustrious Month Hall of Fame. I can't think of a month more deserving of the honour.

What can I tell you about June? Well, she's beautiful and she smells great. How's that for starters? June rules over absolutely the best part of the year, when the trees leaf out and the grass greens up. Every day, it's like someone with a big brush dabbed a little more green paint on the canvas.

But even if you were blindfolded, you would know June is around. There is only one word to describe what a stretch of pasture smells like after a spring rain or a lilac tree in full bloom. That word is June. June is an olfactory factory.

We are close in age, but June is more mature than me in many ways. Other months can be unpredictable, fickle, even vindictive. (I can see you snickering over there, March.) But June? June is reliable. She is warm and friendly. People light up when she enters the calendar.

I'm not sure what it is about June that I like the most, but it might well be her even temper. June is rarely too hot or too cold. The sixth of 12, June is the middle child of the month family. She's the peacemaker. She seeks consensus. She sets an example that other months can only hope to emulate. Oh, she knows how to get tough – some hail here, a tornado there – but she calms right down once the insurance adjusters arrive.

Everybody wants to be around June. Sweden, Denmark, Argentina, Romania and the United States all have their flag days in June. I personally don't know what a flag day is, but if it's on Google, it's safe to say it's pretty darned important. Do you feel like celebrating the independence of Kenya? Well, there's only one day a year you can do that, and it's in June.

Countless celebrities were born in June: Mike Tyson, Angelina Jolie, John Cusack. Ron Wood and Alanis Morissette are both musicians and both were born on June 1. Isn't that ironic?

Father's Day is in June. Imagine getting presents simply for sowing your seed. It's the best thing since farm subsidies.

June has a rich place in history. Custer's Last Stand was in June. D-Day was in June. Winston Churchill gave his famous "finest hour" speech in June. In June of 1178, five monks from Canterbury witnessed an explosion on the moon. (What they were doing there, they wouldn't say.) Salem hung its first witch in June of 1692. By July, the specialty shop Just Pointy Hats was closed.

June is the most popular month of the year for weddings. In fact, she gets her name from the Roman goddess Juno, the patroness of marriage. Juno is the wife of Jupiter – and also, oddly enough, the sister of Jupiter. So she's very family-oriented. I'm sure if you approached a family having a picnic in the park on a fine June day and told them this, they would be very grateful for the information.

Did you know that Juno could throw lightning bolts like her husband? How cool is that? Everybody loves a nice electrical storm.

June is busy. She has a lot to get done. That's why she stays up so late. June contains the longest days of the year. In fact, each day of June is slightly longer than the one before it, all the way to the 21st. If you're afraid of the dark, June is a good month to hang out with. Go far enough north and there's no night at all. If you're a light sleeper, you might resent June for being so bright. But think of all the electricity you're saving.

A bit of a magician, June is. She starts out as a spring month, then transforms into a summer month. How does she do that? It's amazing.

I hate to pick on someone for their size, but you can't help but notice how short June is, having only 30 days. In comparison, January is 45 days long. But if you worked as hard as June, you'd need a rest, too. Is it any coincidence that June is the last month of the school year? I submit to you that there is no better feeling in life than leaving school on the day before summer vacation. It is the essence of freedom. Riding your bike home in the June sunshine, spreading a blanket on the lawn, and realizing four hours into summer that you're already kind of bored – now that's special.

Kind, creative, unique; she is all of that and more. Please join me in welcoming the newest member of the Month Hall of Fame: June!

(Prolonged applause.)

"Thank you, July. Well, I hardly know what to say. I'll just start with this: In your face, February!"

June 5, 2010

Office hypothermia claims another victim

A local man is being remembered as a good worker following his death this week from office hypothermia.

Bud Jones, an editor at the Chronicle Herald Journal, a semi-weekly newspaper in Middleton, Saskatchewan, was found at his desk three days after his family reported him missing. He was 54.

Sources say the temperature in the office is not sufficient to sustain human life.

"Everything seemed normal when I saw him on Monday," said Janine Benice, the paper's administrative assistant. "It was cold in the office, like usual, but Bud was at his desk, trying to keep warm, which is what we do here."

It was only after Mr. Jones failed to move for two more days that his colleagues became concerned.

"I thought he was catching up on some paperwork," said Mr. Jones' supervisor, Helen Peron.

Arts reporter Samantha MacEwan said she regretted not checking on her co-worker when he failed to reply to several routine emails. "I was going to go over there a few times, but that would have meant taking off my blanket, and I just didn't want to feel that blast of cold air."

The grim reality set in when a member of the office janitorial staff asked Mr. Jones to lift his feet so she could mop under his desk. That's when she noticed an icicle hanging from his nose.

Paramedics were called, but it was too late to revive the senior staffer.

Office workers, who spend their breaks in their vehicles in the parking lot with their heaters on, were said to be traumatized by the sight of Mr. Jones being wheeled out of the building in his office chair because his body was frozen and couldn't be placed on a stretcher.

Typical of many offices, the Chronicle Herald Journal's air conditioner runs full out in the summer. As a new revenue source to make up for declining advertising sales, a storage room is rented to the local ice cream shop, Lick 'n' Shiver.

Meanwhile, colleagues praised Mr. Jones for his innovative approach to coping with a cold office.

"I used to think he drank, like, way too much coffee, but he was actually just filling his mug with boiling water so he could bend his fingers for typing," said reporter Jon Charles.

"He was the first to wear a down-filled vest under his down-filled parka," added photographer Melanie Burke. "I use that trick all the time now."

While he had his own body temperature to worry about, Mr. Jones always showed concern for new hires, urging them, "Don't fall asleep; don't fall asleep," when their teeth started chattering.

And then there was his lighter side, as noted by several co-workers. "You know smoke rings? Jonesy would blow air rings on those days when you can see your breath," sportswriter Vince Olivier laughed. "Then there was the time he lost a World Series bet and had to lick the frozen handle of his filing cabinet. He'll be missed, for sure. Once they scrape the frost off his desk, we're gonna light some candles for a makeshift memorial. We were thinking flowers too, but, you know."

According to Statistics Canada, office hypothermia is a growing problem in the workplace, accounting for more than 9,200 lost work days and between five and eight fatalities each year. Less severe cases, where office workers have lost toes and fingers to frostbite, often go unreported.

Officials from Occupational Health and Safety were at the Chronicle Herald Journal most of the week but refused to comment on rumours that the antiquated heating and cooling system in the building contains only one switch marked "too hot" for the winter and "too cold" for the summer.

Meanwhile, the family of Bud Jones has set up a GoFundMe campaign. By late yesterday, it was halfway to its goal of $50.

June 14, 2017

Fall is not happening, fall is not happening

This is the time of year when I start looking for that first traitor leaf. It'll be hiding in an otherwise verdant tree, all yellow and sickly, just itching to let go and drift to the ground.

Surrendering without a fight; what a terrible example to set for the others.

Some entire trees can't wait to give in to f-f-fall. (I can't even say the word.) All it takes is a hint of cool air and a glimpse at the calendar for them to turn their bark on summer. Elm? Ash? Larch? I'm not sure which, but there is a certain type of tree that fills fast with traitor leaves, gives up prematurely and exposes its naked, stickly self to the rigours of winter – and all before the middle of September. Gee, thanks for coming out.

The first yellow leaf is the canary in the coal mine of the seasons, inconvenient proof that – and you didn't hear this from me – WINTER IS COMING.

Faced with that incontrovertible fact, there is only one logical response: denial. In fact, denial is Stage One of the five stages of fall. When the evening air has that little nip in it, tell yourself, "What a refreshing change from all that nice weather." If the sun is setting sooner than it used to, blame the clouds. If the nights seem longer and darker, it might be a lunar eclipse. If you start seeing leaves on the lawn that weren't there the week before, consider the possibility that they aren't real leaves but stunt leaves rehearsing scenes for a football movie.

When denial is your friend, there's no such thing as fall. It's summer all year round. Every day is sunny and warm. The wind is moderate. The UV rating is low. The probability of precipitation is 20 per cent. You can expect a mix of sun and clouds with highs near 25 degrees. Ah, bliss. But wait. What's this? A cool breeze? Can you lend me your sweater? I donated all of mine to cold people.

Denial not working for you? Here's one tactic that will whisk all your worries away: squat under your favourite tree. As the leaves drift down upon your head, hug your knees to your chest, rock gently and repeat: "This is not happening, this is not happening."

Oh, who am I kidding? Denial is just about the stupidest thing you can use for a coping strategy. I'm just so enraged right now I can't think straight. Didn't we just get through another endless, mean, unforgiving winter? Wasn't it spring, like, two days ago? Why did I even bother putting the mitts and tuques away? I suppose it's not too soon to start hunting for the sidewalk salt. What a ridiculous part of the world to live in. In case you didn't notice, I'm entering Stage Two, anger, and I'm not happy about it. I'm going to let loose with a primal scream. I'm going to break things. I'll start with this stupid leaf rake. No, I'll need that. I'll kick something. I'll kick this tree. Ouch. That hurt. And it made more leaves fall. Now I'm really mad.

I'll tell you what. If the weather stays decent, I promise to really enjoy it. I won't squander any more beautiful summer evenings watching *Canadian Idol* in the basement. I'll go for long, boring walks. I'll ride my bike. I'll pitch a tent in the backyard and sleep in it. I'll run through the sprinkler. All the things I could have done all summer long but didn't, I'll do now, if only the sun doesn't do anything rash and start setting at suppertime. To appease the weather gods, I'll make burnt offerings on the barbecue. I'll sacrifice a pickerel. I'll be a good person. Just keep the snow away, please?

If all that sounds like Stage Three, bargaining, you're right. Denial's cousin, bargaining attempts to create an alternate reality, one more palatable than, say, frostbite and days of endless night. If we all just pull together and really, really concentrate – and maybe do something nice for Tibet – I bet we can stretch summer out indefinitely. I've seen winter around here. Believe me, it's worth a try.

You see, it's just such a downer to think about what lies ahead: scraping frost off the car windows, plugging in the block heater, shovelling sidewalks. When I think about putting away the garden hose and patio furniture, I want to weep. It's just so unfair. I can't do another six months of freezing cold, I just can't. Clearly, there is no point going on now that I've reached Stage Four, depression.

On the other (frostbitten) hand, maybe this winter won't be so bad. We do get the odd easy one, after all. Once you get used to the cold and endless darkness, winter does have its charms. Nothing is fresher than the air on a clear, cold day. Fewer sights are more impressive than a snowy field in the bright sun, zillions of diamonds sparkling under a stunning blue sky. The weather outside might be frightful, but the fire is so delightful. It's okay to laze the days away. Only in winter can you spend an entire Saturday doing nothing more arduous than stirring chili and not feel guilty about it. Might as well zip up the parka and give in to the warm embrace of Stage Five, acceptance.

Aaah. I feel so much better now. Let winter do its worst. Acceptance will get me through. I'm just a big ball of Zen-like calm. Nothing can get to me. Thanks to acceptance, I can endure anything. At least until December 27. After that there's no denying it. I'm going to get really angry and depressed.

August 30, 2008

Winter traction bullies lord it over the rest of us

Shortly after the first snowfall of the season, I was the victim of tractionism, not once but twice. Tractionism occurs when another motorist prejudges you on the basis of your grip.

It snowed overnight Friday. I had plans to switch to my snow tires on Saturday. I love my snow tires. I swear by them. But first I had an errand to run.

The roads weren't great but my all-season tires were doing fine. As I drove up the ramp onto University Bridge, a white Audi SUV appeared in my rear-view mirror and kept getting bigger.

In a second, he was on my bumper. We were on a single-lane uphill curve, and he seemed to want to let me know that he could get up the ramp twice as fast as I could.

In other words, he had more grip. He was showing off. He was lording it over me. What a bloody tractionist, I thought. I have no patience for tractionists and their white SUV privilege.

They think they're so great, that the rules of the road don't apply to them because they have four-wheel drive and brand-new Polar Driftkings on every wheel.

Let's face it. Our society is dominated by a segment of the population that takes four-wheel drive and traction control for granted, as if every vehicle has such pricey options. They've never gone through winter on a worn-out set of Sears Econogrips – much less with rear-wheel drive, a sandbag in the trunk for weight and fingers crossed.

The irony is that drivers of marginalized models might actually be better drivers. Surely, anyone with half a brain can drive a sophisticated German gunship with a supercomputer that can detect black ice a month away and eliminate wheelspin in two-millionths of a second. But it takes actual skill and experience to categorize the icy ruts in front of you as benign or threatening and to shift into neutral while applying just the right amount of brake-pedal pressure to keep the wheels from locking.

Maybe tractionists should pick on someone who deserves it, like those people who are too lazy to brush the snow off their cars and drive around peering through the little half-moons made by their windshield wipers. Truly, these are the pariahs of the winter driving world.

My second encounter with tractionism that day was near my house. I stopped to turn right. No one was coming, so I proceeded. It took a little longer than usual to get going because of the ice. By then, a speeding Jeep was coming up behind me – its first run of the day, judging by the tufts of snow flying off its roof. Again, I was in the way, less than human, the subject of vehicular profiling, open to persecution by a grip-flaunting bully.

The worst thing is when tractionists get really close and you find yourself accelerating beyond your comfort zone just to satisfy them. I hate myself for doing that but I'd do anything to get away from them.

Later that afternoon, I finally had time to put my own winter tires on. I shall not be haughty. In the cold and slippery months ahead, I vow to show more compassion for the gripless.

For I have a dream. I have a dream that my children will one day live in a nation where they will not be judged by their traction, but by their character. And by the excellent job they do brushing the snow off their cars.

November 14, 2017

Let's warm up by ignoring wind chill

It's winter. Why make it worse? Last night on the TV weather forecast, they showed a map of the province with the various temperatures in all the towns and cities. But the temperatures were way lower than they should have been. That's because this wasn't the *temperature* forecast, it was the *wind chill* forecast. The "warmest" number was -39.

If there's a way to make winter worse, it's by obsessing over the wind chill. When I was a kid, there were cold days and really cold days, and that was it. Wind chill literally had not been invented yet.

Listen, we're in January. That's bad enough. January is the longest month of the year after March. January is not only our coldest month, it's also our most hilarious. The "normal" high for most days in January is -10. Forget that. It's always colder. Always. If -10 were normal, January wouldn't be getting all that hate mail.

Like January, wind chill is always colder than the actual temperature. What is wind chill? In scientific terms, it's the temperature, plus a punch in the face.

A brief history of wind chill

In 2001, human volunteers agreed to enter a refrigerated wind tunnel, according to an article I found on the Environment Canada website entitled "Canada's Role in Developing the Wind Chill Index." "They were dressed in winter clothing, with only their faces exposed directly to the cold. To simulate other factors affecting heat loss, they also walked on treadmills and were tested with both dry and wet faces."

When the wind was turned on, the volunteers began screaming and begging for Mexico, I presume. I like to think they were allowed to escape before they froze their faces off.

From this research, Environment Canada was able to confirm that it feels much colder when the wind is blowing.

How much colder? At -20, a 20 kilometres per hour wind will make it feel like -30. At -50, a 60 kilometres per hour wind will make it feel like -78. I've never been out at -78 but I told a joke at work recently and nobody laughed, so I figure it's the same feeling. Their research completed, Environment Canada has been making winter worse ever since.

Battling our addiction to wind chill

Every media outlet relies heavily on Environment Canada's forecast. We are now addicted to wind chill. Radio hosts and weather personalities can't wait to give you the bad news. There's always that dramatic pause between the temperature and wind chill. "It's -18 . . . but it feels like -38." It's a boast that ups the ante. You'd sound the same saying something like, "We have a large house . . . and a houseboat." Boom! They tell you to wear layers, because you've never heard of such a thing. They remind you to "bundle up." Every time a radio guy says bundle up, you should get a shot of tequila. It would trigger warmth and general hibernation.

Meanwhile, we're encouraged to ignore the temperature and fixate on the "feels like" temperature. This is a mistake. Knowing how cold it is, to the last micro-degree, makes it worse. I know this because the thermometer in my car is flawed. It always reads a degree or two warmer. I wouldn't say it's inaccurate, merely optimistic. I like it that way. When you believe it's -15 rather than -18, you're happier.

Taking a cue from my car, broadcasters should just give us the temperature and wind speed and let us draw our own conclusions. This means -20 + a 20 kilometres per hour wind = pretty bad but not awful. And -30 + a 30 kilometres per hour wind = winter is holding your head down with the heel of its boot.

Or better yet, let them dispense entirely with the details. Here's what the forecast should sound like: "It's winter. Tomorrow it will still be winter. It'll be winter for the foreseeable future. Now here's Gary with the sports."

January 13, 2017

Brother, you'll hate these sisters

I would like to tell you about three sisters I know. I run into each about once a year and they always seem to leave me in a foul mood.

Jan is the eldest. She is very tall and skinny. She has thin, red lips and a pale complexion. She has white hair with a black streak through it. She's often mistaken for notorious dog-napper Cruella de Vil. No one knows how old Jan is but she's in excellent physical condition. In fact, she gives you the impression that she will live forever.

Jan is angry most of the time. I suspect she's bitter about all the attention lavished on the baby of the family, Dez. Everyone loves Dez. He's generous. He's effervescent. He's fun to be around. He's the life of the party. He's not perfect, mind you. He's fairly loud and abrasive. He's hyperkinetic. And he can be just as dark as Jan. Of course, everyone overlooks his faults because he means well. "That Dez, what a guy," people say. "Can't wait to meet him again."

Naturally, this drives Jan crazy. "What's he got that I haven't got?" she likes to say. The answer is, "Everything," but no one is going to tell Jan that. Most people who meet Jan say she's the coldest person they know. She usually starts the year returning all the gifts she got for Christmas. You don't want to get her mad. Her temper is fierce. When she gets in a bad mood, it can last for weeks.

Even a few minutes with Jan seem like a few hours. As a result, she is a terrible house guest. Do not invite her over. Once you let her in, she won't leave. It doesn't matter how badly you want her to go, she won't do it. Some people have tried giving huge hints, actually going so far as to put their parkas and boots on when they're around her. Others have been known to take trips to Mexico to avoid her. That works for a while, but she's always waiting for them when they get back.

Jan is determined, I'll say that for her. She's very thorough. She has an extensive collection of snow globes. She seems to like staying inside and reading. She's pretty good at sports, particularly hockey, figure skating and skiing. She likes tobogganing, although it's often difficult convincing anyone to go with her. She's also a big fan of NFL football, especially the playoffs.

Some people think Jan is misunderstood. She's not so bad once you get used to her, they say. As her supporters point out, it's not unusual for Jan to suddenly show her warmer side once in a while. This may be true, but she always reverts to her old self. Personally, I dread Jan.

Feborah is the shortest of the three sisters. She has red hair. She's slightly more attractive than her older sister. She's small, but she's wiry. Her handshake is surprisingly firm. She has long, sharp fingernails. You wouldn't want to wrist wrestle with Feborah – she could put you on your knees.

Feborah is very fond of Jan and does her best to emulate her. Feborah can be just as aloof, for instance. There are times when you can hardly tell the two apart. But those close to Feborah say it's just an act. Deep down, she's a bit of a softy. She's not as pessimistic as Jan, for instance. She has a slightly sunnier disposition. On the other hand, she can be very moody. With Jan, at least you know what to expect. Feborah keeps you on your toes. One day she can be your best friend, the next it's like she's out to get you.

Feborah is not a party animal like Dez, but she does like to have some fun – in an eccentric way. She gets positively wacky around Groundhog Day. She's always the first to see if Wiarton Phil or Punxsutawney Willie or one of those dopey rodents has seen its shadow. There's no better way to tell if spring is around the corner – other than rolling the dice, of course. She also loves awards shows, particularly the Grammys and Oscars. But Feborah's favourite occasion is Valentine's Day. She considers herself very romantic, which means she likes to receive flowers and candy. I can put up with Feborah, but only because she doesn't hang around for long.

Mara, third oldest in the family of 12, is just as tall as Jan but she's a little heavier and has a bad complexion. She has green eyes and dirty blond hair. She has piercings through her nose and bottom lip. She has a tattoo of the Roman god of war on her left shoulder. She often goes on fad diets, fasting or eating no meat on Fridays.

Mara is very hard to get along with. Feborah's mood swings seem mild in comparison. She can be laughing and happy one minute and furious the next. You have to walk on eggshells around her. Years ago, suspecting some sort of bipolar disorder, the family tried to convince Mara to see someone about her mood swings, but she insisted she was fine.

Mara gets excited about St. Patrick's Day but usually overdoes it and gets even crankier afterwards. She also claims to love the spring equinox, but some years she ignores it entirely.

Given her brittle personality, Mara has trouble making friends. She spends a lot of time watching TV. She follows the U.S. college basketball finals and pre-season Major League Baseball. No wonder she's depressed.

Jan, Feborah and Mara remind me a bit of the witches in *Macbeth* – those "secret, black and midnight hags." Sounds harsh, but, believe me, you don't want to deal with those girls if you can help it. Luckily, the rest of the family isn't as bad. In fact, there are three other sisters who are real sweethearts.

Their names are April, May and June. I'm looking forward to seeing them again. Boy, am I ever.

January 26, 2008

Last one to Mexico, turn out the lights

There are two groups of people going to Mexico this winter: everyone I know and everyone I don't know. Of course, I'm exaggerating. It's not literally everyone. It's just everyone who isn't going to Varadero or Puerto Plata. Oh, don't I sound like the seasoned winter vacationer, just throwing those names around? I'm not, though. I learned that Varadero is in Cuba and Puerto Plata is in the Dominican Republic by reading the travel section in Saturday's paper.

Pouring over the ads (and I do mean pouring – I spilled my coffee on them), I couldn't help but notice an amazing phenomenon. Apparently, you can pay someone a certain amount of money and they will fly you to a place where exposed flesh won't freeze in less than 30 seconds. When you get there, you can do what pleases you – sit on a beach and drink beer that comes in a clear bottle with a wedge of lime stuck in the top or . . . or . . . I'm not sure what else. Everything I know about sun spots I learned from Corona commercials. If I glanced at another woman on the beach, my spouse would likely squirt lime juice in my face. And that's the limit – the Outer Hebrides – of my travel knowledge.

Almost half a century on the planet and I've compressed far more snow than sand under my feet. It puts one at a disadvantage in an era when everyone goes to Mexico all the time. It's amazing there's anyone left on the street, really. If they're not packing to go, they're already there or they're just getting back.

As a media junkie, I've developed a kind of Mexican radar. It's like when you buy a Kia, you start seeing them everywhere. I might be the last human in Saskatoon who has never been to Mexico but I instantly sense when someone else has. The minute a local radio or TV personality isn't on the air at their usual time, I know what's up. They're quietly just not there for a week. Then they're back, lightly toasted, looking like the cat that ate the tamale.

None of this should even be possible. Nothing moves when it's frozen, and in winter on the Prairies, we're just human ice cubes. And yet, these blocks of motionless molecules find their way onto aircraft – a miracle invention in itself, something too heavy to lift that lifts itself into the air and, my God, flies – and they travel to a different climate in a matter of hours. And all it takes, other than the will to do it, is money.

Hence the ads. Cozumel, Mayan Riviera, Punta Cana. (Punta Cana? Can you say that in a family newspaper?) Please note that I have no idea where these places are. Until today, I thought Los Cabos was a stolen taxi.

Most of the ads I see have the term "All Incl" on them. Even I know what this means – everything you eat and drink is prepaid for. I can conceptualize the idea, but it's as abstract to me as the speed of light. Likewise the "swim-up suite." Your room opens onto the pool. You slither out of bed in the morning, head pounding from an all-inclusive hangover, and slip into the water – millions of years of evolution replayed instantly, in reverse.

Intrigued, I did do some research on Mexico. On a map, you see that it's located at the bottom of North America, a funnel-shaped country with a kind of blob on the end that hooks to the right. Upside down, it looks like a dog bending over to get a sniff of something – New Orleans, perhaps. If it started licking Nogales, you'd scold it.

Mexico has coasts on the Pacific Ocean, the Gulf of Mexico and the Caribbean Sea. Each has a beach, I assume. And each beach contains people worth getting spritzed with citric acid for looking at. Makes me cry a little just thinking about it.

Far off the west coast are the Revillagigedo Islands. There used to be a salad dressing called Revillagigedo Islands; it never caught on.

But tourism did. In 2008, about 22 million people went there. In other words, everyone in Saskatchewan went 22 times. The thing that gets me about frequent Mexico vacationers is the casual way they treat the country – like it's just part of their own backyard. They don't even call Puerto Vallarta Puerto Vallarta. It's "PV." When they hear someone is planning a trip, they're like, "PV or Cancun?" Then it's "Where you staying? The Barcelo La Jolla de Mismaloya? Oh yeah, that's awesome. Great ice maker on the fifth floor beside the fire extinguisher. Say hi to Manuel at the desk. He has a lazy eye. Wife's name's Maria."

Of course, when you've been to Mexico 80 or 90 times, you seek out the hidden gems. Still, it doesn't matter what place you mention – Minatitlan, Apatzingán, Ciudad Mante – the Mexperts have been there. "Tenosique, eh? There's a great little chocolate shop off Calle de Santuario. One of the best Tejates you'll get anywhere. It's owned by a couple from Wynyard." Oh, shut up.

But I do wish you well on your vacation. And to make you feel even better, I've read that tap water in Mexico is now safe to drink. Have lots and lots of it as soon as you land. And say hi to Montezuma for me.

February 13, 2010

Chapter 3

—

Undecorating Christmas

With its unique and sometimes bizarre traditions (kissing under a poisonous weed!?!) Christmas suits me perfectly. It's a season of stark contrasts – rich and poor, light and darkness, cold and warmth, buying and returning. I was a Christmas-loving kid, and I had no choice in the matter. When you have five older brothers and sisters and a mother who worships the ground that Good King Wenceslas walks on, your love of the season is bound to be deep and crisp and even.

Every year, I knew Christmas was coming when the music started. On the first Sunday of Advent, my mom dropped the record player's needle into the crackling grooves of a Nat King Cole LP, and the race was on. Driven by caffeine and cigarettes, my mother sewed, washed walls and vacuumed into the night. She was a commodore in the kitchen, launching armadas of cookie sheets and pie plates and covering every counter and tabletop with treats that absolutely could not be eaten before Christmas. Oh, how I resented you, Advent, you no-fun, four-week endurance test.

And then, for stark contrast, there was my dad, who didn't much like Christmas at all – at least, the tumult and commercialism. Not to mention all the ooey-gooey goodwill stuff that threatened to soften his hard shell. And he was thrifty. It must have driven him crazy seeing his wife spend enough on butter and whipping cream to run the furnace for the winter. Maybe that's why he kept turning the thermostat down. But the poor man didn't stand a chance. It would have been easier to put the snow back in the clouds than to resist Christmas.

For years, the highlight of our family's Christmas celebrations was listening to a wonderful CBC recording of Alan Maitland's Christmas readings. Our favourites were Stephen Leacock's *Hoodoo McFiggin's Christmas*, Frederick Forsyth's *The Shepherd* and O. Henry's *The Gift of the Magi*.

After the traditional feast of traditionally overdone roast beef and an unseemly quantity of baking, we would settle down and listen. The quiet, communal act of absorbing those stories erased the excesses of the season and put everything into perspective. Simply looking at each other's faces while we laughed and cried created a sense of family togetherness that no amount of shopping and wrapping could ever match.

By now, those stories are in my marrow. I'm a repeat offender when it comes to stealing O. Henry's awesome alliteration and echoing Leacock's ironic understatement.

Now that my parents are gone, I realize there always was a middle ground between my mother's love of Christmas and my father's mistrust. It's in that space that my Christmas columns reside – childlike excitement tempered by a niggling suspicion that maybe we're all being hoodwinked.

It's beginning to look . . . don't say it

Have you noticed how excited everyone is about the Grey Cup this year? It's amazing. Stores are reporting record-breaking sales of Grey Cup lights and yard ornaments. Some people started decorating well before the Eastern semifinal, for goodness' sake.

Half my block has been lit up nightly for the past two weeks in anticipation of the big game. Many of the lights are blue, which suggests a lot of support for the Winnipeg Blue Bombers, although more than a few eavestroughs are draped in the traditional red lights of the Calgary Stampeders. It certainly looks festive. There are Grey Cup wreaths on doors. On the roof of one house stands a jolly-looking offensive lineman all decked out in red and white. More than a week ago, I saw a Grey Cup tree in someone's living room. I couldn't believe it. Either some people are whacked in the head or they really must love the CFL.

Each year, Grey Cup celebrations start a little earlier. I'm worried about how over-commercialized it's getting. Are we forgetting the true meaning of the game? When I was a kid, excitement about the Grey Cup didn't begin until well after November 11. That seemed reasonable. Grey Cup is a pretty intense time, what with all the cooking and cleaning and decorating and baking and shopping and buying and consuming and purchasing and spending that goes along with it. Why prolong it? Why put yourself through the wringer for six weeks when three or four provide as much Grey Cup cheer as most people can stand?

I love the game as much as anybody, but you have to admit it's a pretty stressful time, what with all the social obligations: the visiting, the house guests, the office parties. ("Honey, does the home jersey look good with these pearls?") It started out as a simple, beautiful celebration of professional football. Now people agonize over the details, setting standards for themselves that are impossible to achieve. Grey Cup etiquette alone could fill a book:

- Dear Miss Manners: Should I give my boss a Grey Cup gift or would he get the wrong idea?

- If I've only been seeing my girlfriend for three months, should I splurge on jewellery or go with a sausage-and-mustard basket?

Whatever happened to the days when you could simply stick a wreath on the door, pour a glass of beer nog and relax with the family? Some of my fondest childhood memories are of gathering with my brothers and sisters in the rumpus room to watch our favourite TV specials: *Miracle at the 34-Yard Line* and *How the Grinch Stole the Grey Cup*, starring Tony Gabriel.

Those days are over. When the neighbours started putting up their lights around Halloween, I knew I was in trouble. Once my kids noticed the houses all aglow with gridiron cheer, the nagging was relentless.

"Daddy, when can we put up our Grey Cup lights?"

"Daddy, when can we put up our Grey Cup lights?"

"Daddy, when can we put up our Grey Cup lights?"

I finally gave in. It was still too soon, but I found a way to rationalize it – the weather was simply too good to waste. If I waited any longer, I'd be hanging by my tongue on an aluminum ladder at -40 and cursing myself for procrastinating.

So, for the first time ever, I started putting up my lights long before Grey Cup Eve. The first night didn't go so well. I was alone with the kids, and the only time I had to work was the 40-minute window between the end of supper and the start of bath time. I located the lights, carefully stored under the deck last spring. Getting the tangles out in the dark took about 25 per cent of my time. Finally, I plugged in the first string to make sure it worked. A spark erupted from the outlet and one of the lights exploded. Smoke coiled up into the crisp night air.

"I don't want you to die, Daddy," said one of my kids.

I assured him I was fine, though I secretly wondered if it was a bad omen. Discarding the festive daddy-killer string of lights, I got out the other set and started putting it on the porcupine-prickly spruce tree on the west side of the house. Ever notice how the stupid clip that comes attached to each stupid light is practically useless? They have two positions: "not open enough" and "oops, I broke another one." I fought with the stupid clips for a few stupid minutes before giving up and resorting to stupid twist ties. Much better. But by now, half my time had elapsed and my kids were well and truly bored with the entire adventure. To amuse themselves, they started indulging in their new hobby – tormenting the dog. A pattern thus developed: (a) prick self with spruce needle, (b) curse under breath, (c) yell at kids to stop waving at dog with stick, (d) prick self with spruce needle.

By the end of my allotted decorating time, I wasn't exactly basking in the joy of the Grey Cup season. On the other hand, I had one small tree finished days ahead of schedule. Best of all, I was finally part of the crowd. I'd joined the throng of fans who suffer from premature celebration.

Merry Grey Cup, everyone!

November 24, 2001

The Fillmores branch out at Christmastime

In an ordinary, working-class neighbourhood in an ordinary, working-class town lived the Fillmores. The Fillmores were ordinary, too, just a little larger and louder than most of the families around them.

The Fillmores loved Christmas in all the ordinary ways: the gifts, the food, the decorations. But the Fillmores also loved one Christmas thing that was extraordinary: they cut down their own tree.

Rather than buy one from a perfectly good tree lot, rather than order a perfect tree from the Wish Book, they had a "Christmas tree hunt."

It might have been Mr. Fillmore's idea – a way to share his love of the outdoors with his offspring and to give them a sense of self-reliance. Or maybe he hated paying full price for a tree when the North was full of them.

Or it might have been Mrs. Fillmore's idea – a way to get the kids out from underfoot. The mother of six would have relished a day of peace and quiet to bake shortbread, catch up on her smoking and play Bing Crosby LPs.

Whoever had the idea, it went over like gangbusters. Little Willy Fillmore, for one, loved the Christmas tree hunt as much as Slinkys and Spirographs. He always spent the night before waterproofing his lace-up horsehide moccasins. This made them extra slippery, which was perfect for sliding down a country lane while holding onto a truck's tailgate. Anything more fun than that was simply beyond Little Willy's imagination.

Another highlight was the campfire lunch the Fillmores always planned, a simple meal for simple folk consisting of raw garlic sausage roasted over an open fire. Tongues of flame would lick at the dripping fat as the meat chunks hissed and popped and twitched on their sticks. Even the sulphuric effluent of a nearby pulp mill couldn't spoil the aroma.

Dessert usually consisted of hot chocolate from a vacuum-sealed container. But one year, they splurged on a realistic English plum pudding from the grocery store. Wrapped in red plastic and tied with a bow, it was a wonder to behold, a little bowling ball dressed for a night on the town.

The year of the plum pudding was also the year of the "whiskey jacks," bold and handsome birds that you could feed by hand. It might have been Jed Fillmore who got the idea to soak the plum pudding in rum – moisture being the only thing it lacked – and feed it to the whiskey jacks.

Wildlife lovers that they were, the Fillmores found tremendous joy in watching the birds gobble the plum pudding and create eccentric flight paths through the trees. If only more families could appreciate the wonders of the natural world.

Their laughter still echoing in the forest, the Fillmores finally got down to work, for there was a lot to do. The parents needed a tree for their living room, one for their deck and one for their rumpus room. The older Fillmore kids who were already married needed trees of their own. Even some of the in-laws sometimes placed orders.

All afternoon, the Fillmores did exaggerated knee-to-chin walking steps through thigh-deep snow, crossing meadows to find the perfect tree. But these were wild trees. No one trimmed them as they grew. No one watered them in dry years. None was perfect. Simple and honest trees they were. But majestic? Not really.

"Here's a good corner tree," Mr. Fillmore would call out, saw at the ready.

By "corner tree," he meant it was skinny.

"Good wall tree here," he'd say, ever the salesman. This was a tree with a flat side. Maybe his feet were getting cold.

Darkness came early that time of year (but it always comes early, doesn't it?) and before they burned their daylight, the Fillmores loaded their trees and aimed their truck in the direction of the huge pot of chili Mrs. Fillmore would have ready for them.

Back home, they jabbed each tree into the snowbank beside their driveway and tried to remember, now in the dark, which tree was whose.

In truth, it was a rather homely collection of evergreens. It could not have been perfection that the Fillmores sought on their Christmas tree hunts – not with crooked trees, trees with bare spots in the middle, trees that rained needles whenever someone walked by.

Not a single one looked like the kind of tree you could buy from the Wish Book. By the time you finished cutting off the bad bottom half of a sturdy eight-footer, you might be left with a table tree. "So much the better," the Fillmores thought. "We need a little one downstairs for the drum lights."

Back inside the house, the family thawed out. Through the din of laughter and the tap-tap-tap of spoons hitting chili bowls, the kids recounted the day's events to an always-impressed Mrs. Fillmore while Mr. Fillmore sat back in his quilted vest and beamed with satisfaction.

Sadly, the tree hunt tradition came to an end, as all things must. Years later, who knows what the Fillmores really found in the forest on their annual tree-hunting trips the week before their Christmases. But you couldn't be far wrong if you thought that maybe, just maybe, it was something more perfect than a perfect tree.

December 23, 2012

'Tis the season of truly inspired lunacy

Is Christmas the most wonderful time of the year or just the most strange?

What other occasion would force men of goodwill to climb ladders in the dark and risk their lives to affix electrical lights to the edge of their eavestroughs? Could Canada Day inspire such lunacy? Mother-In-Law's Day? Labour Day? No. Only Christmas has that power.

As we speak, there may very well be a dead tree in your living room. Likely, it's marinating in a pot of water in order to make its needles last 15 days instead of 11. The tree is decorated, of course. Maybe with a string of popcorn, which no one is allowed to eat. Or candy canes, which no one is allowed to eat. Why not put out a bowl of burned-out Noma lights for the kids to snack on?

Feeling romantic? Let your love grow by kissing someone under a poisonous weed, such as mistletoe.

Christmas is inexplicable, I realized while reading Sue Wollard's book *Remembering That Christmas.* Did you know that Christmas has a checkered past? Before Christmas was invented, the pagans had all the best parties. It was hard for early Christians to compete, so they did the next best thing: they stole the best parts of the Roman festivals of Saturnalia and Kalends and threw a birthday party for Christ. If Christmas were a student, it would be expelled for plagiarism.

Christmas isn't just lacking in originality, it's also shockingly violent. Rumour has it that Nicholas, the fourth-century Bishop of Myra, brought three young boys to life "after their bodies had been cut up and pickled in brine to be used as a substitute for bacon."

Times were hard in the 300s. But Bishop Nicholas was a great guy who gave to the poor, which is why he inspired the legend of Santa Claus. One man the future St. Nick helped had three daughters. He was too poor to pay their dowry, so the Bishop dropped gold coins down the man's chimney. Wouldn't you know it? The coins rolled right into the girls' stockings, which were set out to dry. Naturally, it makes perfect sense to celebrate the giving of gifts by observing St. Nicholas Day. We don't, however. St. Nicholas Day is December 6. Why do we celebrate 19 days later on the 25th? Because no one would have their shopping done in time.

Christmas is the perfect season to feel guilty about not writing to your friends more often. To heap on even more pressure, Christmas cards were invented. The very first one, according to the British Museum, was created by William Egley in 1842. Egley planned to get his card finished by 1841, but he was too busy, what with all the shopping he had to do.

Some traditions have sadly been overtaken by technology. Yule logs used to be a cherished part of Christmas. They were lit on Christmas Eve and allowed to burn for 12 days. In Scandinavia, the log was decorated before it was dragged from the forest. If you encountered a family pulling their log, it was good luck. I wish I'd known that the day we got our new furnace delivered this fall. I would have stuck a couple of ribbons on the half-ton and done a little jig.

Food is a particularly harrowing part of Christmas. People in Europe marked Advent by eating a sweet bread called Christollen. It was covered with white icing to make it look like a baby in swaddling clothes. I like babies as much as the next guy, but let's keep them off the menu, folks.

Christmas food has a habit of being unpalatable. Candied rind? Walnuts? Sickly sweet cherries? Chocolates with orange cream filling? All defy eating. Sugar plums not only contain no plums, they contain no food at all, unless you include the clove stuck on the end. In some cultures, it's believed that sugar plums dance through children's heads because they cause hallucinations.

The tradition of inedible Christmas food may have started in Northern Europe. In the winter, farmers could afford to feed only their best animals. They slaughtered the rest, which caused some storage problems in the days before refrigeration. The most logical solution was to make a "plum awful" pudding from the surplus meat. It was a thick soup of mutton or beef with raisins, currants and spices added to make it truly horrible. Mincemeat had a similar origin: leftover meat with dried fruit cooked in pies that were cleverly shaped like Jesus' crib to make you think about eating infants.

In the days of meat pudding, it was important to keep people's minds off food, which is why carols were invented. I finally studied the words to

Jesus Christ the Apple Tree. It goes like this: "The trees of nature fruitless be, compared to Christ the apple tree" and "This fruit doth make my soul to thrive it keeps my dying faith alive." But if you can compare Christ to an apple tree, doesn't that invite other equally indelicate culinary comparisons? How about "This food doth make my soul pay homage, to Christ the one true Grand Fromage" or "The foods of spice you'll need a lotta, to equal Jesus the Big Enchilada."

Christmas is full of odd contradictions. It's the time of year when adults can act like children, when things go on sale after you need them, when you carefully wrap gifts only to see the paper torn off, when you put presents in stockings that are impossible to wear.

A virgin birth? A baby king? Christmas is the most wonderful, strange time of year.

December 20, 1997

You better watch out, I'm telling you why

This just in: Christmas can kill you. It's true. A study released this week by researchers at the University of California at San Diego proves that you're most likely to die on three particular days of the year: December 25, December 26 and January 1.

This is no casual guesstimate. A team of sociologists studied death certificates of 53 million people over a 28-year period. What they found is enough to curdle your eggnog: deaths on those three days are 11.9 per cent higher than normal for cardiac causes and 12.2 per cent higher for all other causes, such as Ferrero Rocher overdoses and random sleighings. The information has been forwarded to the Grinch Institute at Mount Crumpit for further study.

According to researchers, the causes of increased mortality have nothing to do with cold weather, diet or slow cashiers. It seems that people avoid going to the doctor over the holidays because they're too busy or too far from home. There's also a suggestion that the quality of care might not be as good as it is at other times of the year. This appears to be supported by another study that found the mortality rate for cardiac patients in the U.S. was 22.5 per cent over the holidays but only 20.5 per cent the rest of the year. More gravy, anyone?

I'd always wondered why Christmas made me feel funny inside. Is it joy? Or is it the feeling that I'm being stalked by a menace?

As a person beset by freak accidents, I've got to be doubly careful this time of year. It started in childhood. While all the other kids were getting routine scraped knees and such, I was parked on my Mustang bicycle, spinning the handlebars around and around, seeing how close I could put my face to the whirring flash of chrome before . . . OUCH! I wouldn't even remember that day if I didn't still have the chip in my front tooth to remind me. But that bike wasn't done with me yet. Those same handlebars came down on the big toe of my bare foot one summer, causing the nail to turn black and slough off several weeks later. (I mailed the specimen to my brother as a joke.)

Established in childhood, the mishaps kept coming. It's not unusual, for instance, to blow out your knee when you're skiing. But it is when you are cross-country skiing. I happened to be a reckless 18-year-old and decided to shoot down a steep hill with my cross-country skis on, so you can't really say I had an accident, as such. What I had was more like an *inevitable.* But the freaky thing is that the skis in question were my Christmas present. Coincidence?

No season is safe for me, unfortunately. Two summers ago, a fun frolic in a city swimming pool turned nasty when my son accidentally poked me in the eye with his razor-sharp finger nail. The eye specialist assured me the blurring would go away eventually.

The doc was quite impressed with the depth and shape of the scratch, by the way; ragged tearing of that sort is most often caused by run-ins with trees, he told me. Evergreen trees.

Having kids invites all sorts of personal injuries. Like the time I decided to go for a spin on my child's scooter and hit a crack in the sidewalk at full speed. I wasn't wearing a helmet but it didn't matter because, after I flew over the handlebars and rolled across the cement, my head was just about the only part of me that remained unscathed. The skin on my leg would grow back eventually, but the rib damage meant that sneezing and coughing were no longer acceptable. Also, for the first two weeks, I could get out of bed in the morning only by slithering off feet first while lying on my stomach. Funny thing is, the kids hardly ever use those scooters. What a shame. They were gifts. Christmas gifts.

Most accidents occur in the home, they say. My home. Three weeks ago, on the last Thursday of November, I decided to slice an onion by using the index finger of my left hand as a cutting board. By the end of the day, something I'd always wondered about had been made clear: when you cut yourself, how do you know whether you really need stitches or if a bandage will do? Believe me, you know. Freshly sewn up and frozen, my finger was back home from the Mediclinic in two hours. Most intriguingly, this particular accident did not occur on any old day, but one I had carefully taken off from work in order to watch football and cook turkey: American Thanksgiving – the official start of the holiday season in the U.S. The holiday season.

Which brings us to the Tree of Death. I've enjoyed a long and cordial relationship with Christmas trees. I've cut them down in the wild and I've purchased them from parking-lot vendors. Never has a tree struck back – until this year. There we were on a pleasant family outing, looking fir the perfect tree at one of the city's best-known tree lots. The Scotch pines looked enticing, so I stood a tall, heavy one up and checked it out. No. Not quite what we wanted. I placed the tree against the fence and turned to go. Just then, it started to move toward me. Gently, it kind of leaned against the side of my head. As it did, it inserted one of its long, straight needles into my ear. In it went, farther than any finger, Q-tip or car key has ever gone before. A sudden, piercing pain shouted out from somewhere inside my head. I recoiled like I'd been stung. The tree stood there looking innocent, practically daring me to sue for pain and suffering. What was the use? There were no witnesses, and the only proof of the assault was the throbbing pain only I could feel. And, really, how could anyone have their inner ear violated by a Christmas tree?

Luckily, there was no blood, and my hearing seemed normal despite the excruciating pain. But who knows? Maybe the needle punched a hole in there somewhere and germs are infiltrating my brain this very minute, marshalling their forces until they're strong enough to launch an all-out attack. I suppose I should go to the doctor to check it out, but I'm just so busy right now – the holidays, you know.

December 18, 2004

But it's Christmas, Grandpa Fillmore

Every once in awhile, Grandpa Fillmore would visit for Christmas.

Was it a time of great excitement for the assorted Fillmore children? It was not, at least not for the youngest.

Little Kimmy Fillmore was always uneasy about this relative stranger who arrived on a cold front in a Ford sedan. The ancient farmer was as skinny as an icicle. He had a sparrow-like face and small, too-pale blue eyes. He wore suspenders and never took off his boots.

Grandpa Fillmore was given Kimmy's room, which turned the boy into a refugee on the downstairs couch. Little Kimmy got revenge by snooping in the codger's luggage, finding odd artifacts like stretchy metal sleeve garters and liver pills.

Little Kimmy and his sister were fascinated by the farmer's deeply furrowed brow. They were driven to hysterics when he ate because his prominent ears cantered up and down on the sides of his head. The harder Kimmy and his sister tried not to laugh, the harder they did – but internally, until it hurt, like suppressing a giant sneeze.

Maybe it was the Dirty '30s that shaped Grandpa Fillmore's character. Maybe hard times took everything he had.

He made no unnecessary expenditures, not of money or warmth or words. He couldn't afford a laugh, couldn't spare a candy. He just sat and smoked his pipe, tucking the spent matches in his pants cuff. Maybe he was saving them for firewood.

Grandpa Fillmore's view of gifts was unusual. He seemed to believe that it was wasteful to give and decadent to receive. So when he got presents on Christmas morning, he put them beside his chair and didn't open them.

Little Kimmy Fillmore couldn't imagine such a thing. A wrapped box was for tearing open with wild abandon before lurching for the next like a desert drifter mistaking sand for water.

It says something about the Fillmore family's love of Christmas that their sometimes-houseguest did nothing to dull the gleam on their garland. It was business as usual: too much food, too many boxes, too hot a house, too much noise and just enough happiness.

Then came the year of the flu, contracted only by little Kimmy Fillmore. He was quarantined on the couch downstairs, feverish and feeling sorry for himself. At least he got out of Midnight Mass. But he had to be alone with Grandpa Fillmore.

Kimmy fell asleep. Only seconds later, it seemed, he was jolted awake by a joyous cacophony. Incredibly, Grandpa Fillmore was laughing heartily upstairs as the various Fillmore children arrived home to discover a mountain of gifts under the tree. The sly fox must have spent a month shopping and wrapping! The trunk of the old Ford must have been stuffed like a goose! With a sense of mischief no one knew he had, Grandpa Fillmore must have snuck the gifts in, no doubt chuckling as he placed them under the tree, maybe even scolding himself like Ebenezer Scrooge: "I don't deserve to be so happy."

Little Kimmy forgot entirely about being sick and grabbed the biggest box with his name on it. He wanted to rip into it but decided to open it slowly to draw out the dizzying anticipation. He even closed his eyes. His plan was to unwrap the gift completely, then relish the full sensory onslaught.

Finally, the moment of discovery was at hand. Little Kimmy opened his eyes . . . and found himself where he had been all along – on the couch with a Christmas fever.

It was a mirage. Grandpa Fillmore, snoring on the chair nearby, hadn't brought presents. But maybe his presence had changed things – in an upside-down way, maybe the ancient farmer could be credited for planting the seed of a wonderful Christmas dream, something he would never know he gave and therefore couldn't take back. This being the season of generosity, let that sentiment prevail.

After a few days, Grandpa Fillmore packed his bag and drove home to his frozen fields. In his suitcase were a wide variety of unopened gifts – with the exception of one box of chocolates, which he never noticed was missing.

December 23, 2017

These are a few of Cam's favourite things

One special thing about the holidays is the traditional airing of the movie *The Sound of Music.*

If you're like me, you can't wait for it to come on TV so you can run screaming from the room with your ears plugged, crying "Make it stop! Make it stop!" Some people adore the story of Maria, a problem nun who falls in love. Needless to say, I don't make a habit of it.

But it does contain some extraordinary songs. One of them, *My Favourite Things*, is particularly timely around Christmas, a crucial season in the acquisition and dispersal of things.

There must have been a commercial for *The Sound of Music* on TV recently because *My Favourite Things* was going through my mind. I was in the garage at the time, and I looked down and spied my anvil on the floor.

"That's it!" I thought. "This is one of my favourite things." I meant it, too. I love that little anvil. It fits the criteria for many things I like. It's heavy for its size, for instance. I like things that are heavy for their size. And I got it cheap – for a song, you might say. And it looks cool, just like the cartoon anvils that were always falling on Wile E. Coyote when I was a kid.

A thought exercise thus presented itself. Could I name a few of my favourite things? What would I pick, and why? I laid out some rules. In the movie, Maria is quick to list crisp apple strudels and schnitzel with noodles. (Coincidentally, they rhyme!) I decided to disqualify a taste or smell. It had to be a thing. And a thing you can hold in your hand, so not your car. Maria liked "Snowflakes that stay on my nose and eyelashes." Poetic, but doesn't qualify.

And how many things should I include? Maria lists around 14. That's her sunny disposition. She likes practically everything. If the song had another verse it might be: "Baroness Schraeder when she's finally dispatched, Nasty Nazis with their plugs wire detached."

But for my game, I limited the number to three. And each had to be a different kind of thing. So not a wrench and a screwdriver, because they're both tools.

In kind and quantity, "things" change as you get older. As a kid, half my toys and games would have been contenders. Things mean less to me now. If there's anything I don't need, it's more stuff.

I began to look around the house. I was amazed at how many things fell short of the top three. I thought it would be hard limiting my list to three things. In fact, it was hard finding that many.

My fishing pictures? Maybe, but my memory can replace them. Nickels? I have containers full of them – they're heavy for their size, after all. But no.

It came down to these few things: My Peasant Chef's Knife from Lee Valley. Notable for not having a stainless steel blade. A gift from my wife. Super easy to sharpen. Cool wood handle. I love my knife. In fact, it knocked out the anvil because they're both tools.

My vintage Handicraft Supplies sign, from a store I spent half my child-hood in. My wife saved it from destruction. It's 15 feet long. There's only one wall in the house where it fits. It makes me happy every time I see it.

My vintage airplane ashtray. A chrome time machine from the 1950s. I had a chance to buy one once, but let it go and instantly regretted it. My wife (yay for wives!) found one years later.

I would like to say that these are a few of my favourite things, but it's more like these are ALL of my favourite things. On one hand, I like the feeling of not being encumbered. On the other, I think I just ruined my chances of getting anything for Christmas.

December 20, 2015

Mrs. Fillmore was the real Christmas expert

Mrs. Fillmore lived with her husband and six children in an ordinary house in an ordinary part of an ordinary city. All the year round, they blended in with every other family in every other way. The exception was Christmas, which Mrs. Fillmore elevated to a status unrivalled by anyone in town regardless of breeding, occupation or credit rating. Mrs. Fillmore loved Christmas. She loved Christmas, even though every year, it would try to kill her.

Her labours started in the fall with a thorough house cleaning: the washing of all the walls and windows, all the fancy dishes in the buffet cabinet – even though they were already clean. Before it even started, the holiday season was trying to consume her to the point of exhaustion. It was all so much. You had to wonder why she did it.

And then it was a sprint to Christmas. The starting line was the first Sunday of Advent when the needle of the record player hit the first holiday record album. With the buttery tones of Bing Crosby drifting into every corner of the house, Mrs. Fillmore got down to business.

She was a force of nature, guided by an unshakeable faith in the reason for the season and driven by stamina that would make Welsh coal miners break down and cry.

By night, powered by Coke, coffee and nicotine, Mrs. Fillmore took on sewing machine marathons and bouts of late-night vacuuming.

By day it was baking. She turned a truckload of flour and sugar into every kind of baked treat worth tasting. Her shortbread cookies were mythical – melt-in-your-mouth butter clouds.

There was Christmas cake, pound cake and matrimonial cake. There were butter tarts and mincemeat tarts and lemon tarts. Raisin cookies, molasses cookies and jam jams. There were peanut butter balls. There were sugar plums, sweet enough to send an electric shock of pain through your teeth.

Mrs. Fillmore even prepared an elaborate treat for a sister in America – candied oranges stuffed with Christmas cake, each in its own glass jar. Before mailing the parcel, she would hurl it down the stairs to the basement. If it didn't jingle, it was ready to ship. Mrs. Fillmore was the only person in Canada to export oranges to California.

Having devoted so much time and energy to Christmas, Mrs. Fillmore cultivated likes and dislikes.

Mrs. Fillmore disliked: Artificial trees. Because they weren't real.

Mrs. Fillmore liked: Blue lights. And not those frosted pale blue lights. They had to be the semi-transparent dark blue ones. These were somehow more reverent.

Mrs. Fillmore disliked: Blinking tree lights. Blinking lights suggested a kind of superficiality that was not in keeping with the season.

Mrs. Fillmore disliked: The word Xmas.

Mrs. Fillmore disliked: The song *I Saw Mommy Kissing Santa Claus*. She did so for two reasons: (1) It gave away the secret. And (2) sex.

Mrs. Fillmore disliked: Form letters. If the card wasn't personalized, you were taking the easy way out.

Mrs. Fillmore disliked: Gift certificates. An abdication of the gift giver's sacred duty to invest time and effort into the giving of an actual thing.

Mrs. Fillmore disliked: The phrase "Happy Holidays." (See Xmas, above.)

And yet, the dislikes were eclipsed by the things Mrs. Fillmore liked about Christmas.

At the top of that list was *Silent Night*. Mrs. Fillmore loved *Silent Night*. No one will ever know how many times she paused from her sewing, cleaning and baking to bask in that glowing line "Round yon virgin mother and child." Mrs. Fillmore loved mothers. She loved babies. Her greatest fear was losing one. Mary did – a sacrifice that renders all others trivial. Mrs. Fillmore's awe at that fact never dimmed.

Which brings us to today, when every theme from every Christmas expert is how to simplify the season, how to get away with doing less.

Doing less? That was a concept as alien to Mrs. Fillmore as artificial trees.

Years before Mrs. Fillmore would sleep in heavenly peace, she recognized the privilege of sacrifice. The hardest-earned rewards are sweeter than sugar plums.

December 23, 2016

Gift exchange spreads the joy

Nothing brings a family together at this special time of year like the never-controversial gift exchange.

Imagine the joy that will emanate from the homes of the tall and the small when they open their presents on Christmas morn and get exactly what they wanted, from pantootlers to fabulous iPod peripherals. Why, the feeling of goodwill that's unleashed by all this generosity could last the entire year, or until the small parts fall into the carpet and the cat eats them.

The Fillmore family was always one to embrace the magic of the gift exchange.

Things were simple at first. With six Fillmore kids and two Fillmore parents, each person could give a gift to each other person. All through the '60s and '70s, gifts were given with generosity and received with gratitude – Slinkys, Rubik's Cubes, Kodak Instamatics. But then the Fillmore boys and girls grew up and went a-courtin' and brought Fillmore in-laws into the fold.

The family grew faster than the hair on a Chia Pet. In a few short years, there was a deafening gaggle of Fillmore grandkids, nieces, nephews and cousins.

As Papa Fillmore said, "Every year Santa has to Fillmore stockings." Everyone laughed heartily. It doesn't take much to amuse a Fillmore.

Bound by tradition, the Fillmores were reluctant to change with the times. But it became more and more challenging for each to buy a gift for the other. It was hard to keep track of who was interested in what. Is Alfie into hockey and Jimmy into string art, or is it the other way around? Sally loved that Hilary Duff CD last year but now she's turned Goth and will only listen to the music of a band called Killerkript Hellkult.

It took weeks to find out who wanted what and months to plan and execute the shopping. And the expense? Oh, it was doable with careful budgeting. But many of the Fillmores were forced to work two or three jobs and live out of boxes near the weir in order to pay for it all.

Once the police started clearing out the hobo village to make way for downtown riverbank development, it was clear the Fillmores would have to find homes and compromise on gift giving. The solution they hit upon was a gift exchanging process where each person has to buy only one gift. It was called a "white elephant gift exchange," or "Yankee swap," though forgetful Fanny-Mae Fillmore kept calling it a "Mexican sidewalk sale."

A random draw determines the order. Person One opens a gift. Person Two has the option of opening a gift as well or "stealing" Person One's gift, and so on. The tradition goes back to the very beginning of gift giving, when the Magi played a game of stealing each other's water as they crossed the desert.

As luck would have it, Cousin Doug brought wizened, taciturn Aunt Alice over on the first year of the event. Doug swears he explained the rules to his mom, but you wouldn't have known it.

She thought the reason she got to go first was because she was the guest of honour.

That feeling was confirmed when she opened a lovely Tim Hortons collectible coffee tin and mug set. She carefully placed it under her chair and gloated.

When Eddie went to "steal" it, Aunt Alice hissed and lashed out. "I knew this wouldn't work," Cassandra said, prying the crone's fingers off her husband's throat. Only a copious amount of rum and eggnog restored the Fillmores to their previous good cheer that year.

Fearing further violence, the Fillmores dropped the idea. How to save money and preserve the traditional values of the season? The Fillmores hit on a new solution. "Let's all give something homemade," someone proposed at a family meeting. A furious fall season of sewing and baking ensued. This time, several of the Fillmores had to take leaves of absence from their jobs to find the time. Mary Ellen, Bob's wife, enrolled in a carpentry course at community college and made bookends with her new radial arm saw. Larry, Mindy's second husband who was on workers' compensation for what he said was a sore back, made a big batch of beer. He drank it while it was still in the primary fermenter, however, and had to brew another. Mitch made delicious venison jerky from the deer he shot while on day parole. Even the tiny Fillmores got involved. Tasha crafted two dozen macaroni mosaics with a little help from her mom who had to stay up until two in the morning three nights in a row despite having a second-degree burn on her thumb from the hot glue gun.

Oh, it was an exhausted Fillmore clan that met that year for Christmas dinner and the homemade gift exchange.

Sleep deprivation, sore joints and the intricacies of TIG welding seemed to dominate the conversation. But the feast was one for the ages. The roast beef, overcooked as only a Fillmore can do, was delicious. The plum pudding positively glowed, its flame fuelled by the finest budget brandy.

As the evening wore on, the old feelings of comfort and joy returned. Uncles chased and tickled giddy toddlers. Aunts cuddled new babies. Grandkids got happily soaked playing football outside in the snow. Dads found time to sneak a cigar on the deck.

Grandparents beamed at the mayhem and merriment they'd founded. The revelry continued with a game of charades that took the clock past midnight. It was fun. So much fun, in fact, that the Fillmores forgot one thing: to open their presents! There was no time now, not with the seniors dozing in their chairs and the kids fast asleep under piles of coats in the bedroom. The only thing to do was take the boxes and gift bags home where they came from. It should have been a disaster. But somehow, while loading their trunks with scrap iron paperweights and homemade best-of CDs from a band called Bloodlet Deathrage, each and every Fillmore agreed: it was the best gift exchange ever.

December 16, 2006

How disposable are thy branches

Breaking up is hard to do, particularly when it's with a tree.

There's a tinder-dry evergreen in the corner of our living room right now blissfully unaware of what horrors await.

The call came in from the governor and the news isn't good. All avenues of appeal have been exhausted. Its time is up. It's a ticking tannenbaum.

The tree has been undecorated for a week now. A puddle of needles is accumulating at its base. It looks naked – strangely enough, more naked than it did when it first came into the house, as if undecorating removes something special and intangible along with the ornaments. Hope, maybe. Or trust.

No relationship is as hot and cold as the one between the Christmas reveller and his tree. You couldn't wait to set it up and decorate it. You played special music for the occasion, perhaps while sipping a nutmeggy concoction of milk and eggs. You assiduously cut a piece from the trunk to expose fresh, moisture-sucking wood, knowing that failing to do so would invite disaster. Perhaps you counted the rings, taking quiet note of the hard years where the rings were close together and the easy years where they were far apart. There's a lesson here. Exactly what, I'm not sure.

After taking pains to make sure it was straight in the stand, you went through bouts of hydration agonization, filling the reservoir with hot water, just like the directions said, to open up the pores. The first time you forgot to replenish the container and found the stump sitting in nothing but air was terribly upsetting, the guilt tremendous. You let it down, man. You let the whole family down.

All those pitched emotions are but a dim memory now. It might as well have happened four months ago, not four weeks ago. The minute that proud fir or pine or spruce no longer gave shelter to the gaudy village of wrapped presents below, it became expendable. Did you forget to plug in the twinkle lights last night? Oh well. Was there water in the base this morning? Maybe. But it's such a hassle to crawl under and check.

The American Dialect Society's latest Word of the Year is "plutoed." Something that's been diminished or stripped of its significance, as the former planet was, is said to have been plutoed. Look up the word in the dictionary and there will be a picture of your undecorated tree beside it.

Ephemeral is another good word. It describes the life span of a Christmas tree lot. Teeming with busy parents and excited kids one day, then abandoned the next. Even on December 24, on the brink of unleashed joy, if you drive by a dark corner of a mall parking lot you'll see an empty tree lot – or worse, one still holding a few unwanted examples on remand, raised and cultivated and harvested and marketed all for naught. Not so much an evergreen as a never-seen. So much sadness.

Are the lows lower than the highs are high? It seems so in January, the month that I fear the most – a vast, windblown, empty month. Note that it seems longer than December. That extra time is January's way of pushing your head down when it stands up after tackling you.

Another kind of tree lot springs up now, the tree disposal lot. It's not unusual to see these drop-off points get their first deliveries on December 26. That's an incredibly grim sight to me. I often wonder about the day-after tree disposers. Do they despise the holidays, taking the very first opportunity to banish the memory of them from their homes? Or maybe they love it all too much. Maybe they were the ones who put their tree up in November and by now it's threatening to spontaneously combust. Either way, you're going to see the Ghost of Christmas Past when you visit the tree dump. Fabulously expensive trees that were oohed and aahed over scant days before are now half-dressed in white garbage bags and sporting nothing but errant strands of tinsel; rich folk passed out after a party.

Disposal is inevitable. But if not at the tree dump, then where? I know someone who slices the limbs off his tree and feeds them into the fireplace. I know it's wood, but that seems somehow cruel. You just don't do that to a friend. You can also throw the thing into the backyard and wait for spring, then haul it to the landfill. Another terribly distasteful option.

Even when you're done with it, it can't be garbage, it just can't. If you had the nerve, you might march right back to the store and demand a refund. "Look at all the needles falling off. Surely there's been a recall. It's clearly defective."

The question of when concerns me most, however. Too soon and you're dishonouring the season. Too late and you're living in the past. No matter how much you loved it, the tree must go – and soon. You don't want your neighbours to think you're eccentric. But wait. Haven't you all been living with dead trees in your houses for the past month? How weird, in itself, is that? It all made sense at the time. It's like some group hysteria took hold. Worrying about what others think seems a bit of a stretch now. There's a lesson to be learned here. People who live in houses shouldn't throw glass ornaments. Or something like that.

January 13, 2007

Chapter 4

A Vow Made in Ink

Two people see each other across a room. It's a crowded room. There are six billion people in it. But these two are made for each other. It's a miracle. They have so much in common that they absolutely, positively have to spend the rest of their lives together. Yes, there will be bumps along the way. But nothing that can't be resolved if only he'd realize she is right.

My crowded room was actually a crowded hallway at the University of Regina. I was waiting in line with a bunch of fidgety extroverts to take an admission test at the School of Journalism and Communications. I looked up from my fascinating shoes to see a tall, beautiful brunette near the door.

Tunnel vision came over me. It was like someone took a pencil and blurred everything around her. Intuitively, I felt something profound, something that went far deeper than any kind of guess or assumption. It went something like this:

"There's no way that girl would ever go out with me."

Five years later, we were married. Lucky, right? I know. I still can't believe it. Why do things work between couples? What happens when they don't? Relationships are a rich and irresistible source of inspiration for columnists. In my case, the only question is how much I can divulge before she kills me.

Writing about marriage is like walking through a forest. You're on a path, a bridal path, let's say. Eventually, you step on some twigs. They are covering a pit. You fall in. Then you write about how you had no idea there was a pit there.

Twigs are the warning signs – you've done something wrong. But if she has to tell you what that is, you're a worse person than she thought you were. The pit is the thing she's upset about. You had no idea until you stumbled into it. Those cupcakes were for the book club. You can't wash a bra that way. You never help me unless you're asked, blah, blah, blah. (Did I just say "blah, blah, blah"? I meant "and so on, and so forth.")

In defence of men, let me say we mean well. In fact, I contend that men are the true romantics. Did you know they spend five times more money on Valentine's Day than women? Chocolate, flowers, dinner, jewellery – they diversify their investment in the hope of positive returns. Men give a lot of thought to what women want. Whether they're right is another question. That's why my father once bought my mother a vacuum cleaner for Christmas.

Women are pragmatists. They put the appropriate life event in the appropriate box at the appropriate time. Then they tape it shut, label it, shelve it and move on. Yes, getting her man is part and parcel of a happy life. But she's not going to stop everything and feed him chocolate-covered strawberries for the rest of her life. No, she's got stuff to do. A career. Babies. Lunch with the girls. Lucky for him, when there are no strawberries, he can still find some beans in the cupboard.

Daily grind wears Russ and Larissa down

Russ and Larissa are nice, normal people. They've been married six years. They have two children. They hold down full-time jobs and are productive, law-abiding members of the community.

Today on What's Love Got To Do With It? we'll examine the little, insignificant, niggling issues that confront Russ and Larissa as they go about their daily lives. As always on What's Love Got To Do With It? our intention is not to find fault with either party – especially the man – but to learn more about how two people who love each other very much can drive each other very much up the wall.

Early on in their marriage, Russ and Larissa divided up the household chores. He would cook and handle the dishes. She would vacuum, clean bathrooms and take amazingly long showers. Neither would do the ironing unless absolutely necessary.

This division of labour continues to the present day, but not without controversy. Sometimes, not often mind you, but sometimes, Russ gets home to find that morning's unrinsed porridge dish on the kitchen counter. It's been sitting all day. The guck is now welded on. "Is it so hard to rinse a dish?" he will mutter under his breath while scrubbing furiously.

Once he complained about this to his wife. She was flabbergasted. From her point of view, it was a case of the pot (unwashed) calling the kettle black.

"You're the non-dish-rinser of all time!" she said. Larissa don't take no guff from nobody. In fact, she's the non-guff-taker of all time.

Larissa, being female, has a thing about bathrooms. The difference between men and women can be summed up thusly: when company is coming, the first thing a man thinks is "I should put some beer in the fridge!" The first thing a woman thinks is "Oh my God, I have to scrub the toilet!"

In a woman's mind, the scrubbing of the toilet earns bonus points in the game of life – points that can be redeemed at any time or place. Sort of like Air Miles.

"You forgot to put gas in the car again," the man will complain to his wife.

"Oh, yeah? Well who do you think cleans the toilets around here?" she will retort.

Newlyweds would call this exchange "a fight" and burst into tears. Experienced married partners call it "a conversation."

Being a man, Russ has no idea what laundry is all about. As a bachelor, he sorted clothes by the day of the week they were last worn. Larissa, he quickly learned, has a much more complicated system. White socks get their own pile. Tea towels get another. Russ once tried to wash white socks and white tea towels at the same time. It's not known what the result was, but Russ is now afraid of the washing machine.

That leaves the dryer. One day when Larissa was out, Russ thought he'd help by loading the dryer. He didn't know that some clothes can be dried and some simply can't. Take the brassiere, for instance. It is a marvel of engineering and architecture. Judging by the strong construction of brassieres, Russ thought they were tough enough to withstand a brief encounter with the dryer. What he didn't know is that brassieres should, if at all possible, be air-dried by the flapping wings of a monarch butterfly. Russ found this out the hard way. Now bras scare him, too.

A bottle of bleach, in a man's hand, is a loaded gun. Most women prefer to put bleach on a high shelf where their husbands can't reach it. One night, after one of their kids had an "accident" in the tub, Russ thought drastic action was needed. He decided to sterilize the entire area with bleach. It was germ warfare.

In war, there are casualties. In this case, some expensive towels were accidentally splashed with bleach. They are now Dalmatian towels. Russ considered this collateral damage, a lamentable but acceptable loss. Larissa did not. She couldn't believe how careless her husband was. Russ, the war hero, plans to avoid the draft the next time.

"Would you mind doing something?" seems to be an innocuous question. In the midst of a January cold snap, it could mean anything. What we're dealing with here is "subtext." Subtext is a way of cussing out your partner without using any bad words. For the past few years, Russ has been winding their car's block heater extension cord around the front licence plate holder. He thought Larissa liked it that way. In reality, she found it annoying. At 30 below, an extension cord has the flexibility of a Chinese dictator. Coiling it is a waste of time. Thus, the question, "Would you mind doing something?" actually means, "You're driving me crazy with that stupid extension cord." Subtext. After years of marriage, it becomes a second language. The question, "Were you thinking of doing something tonight?" isn't a question at all. It means, "I hope you didn't have plans for tonight because I'm watching *Law and Order*."

At this point, you might be wondering what keeps Russ and Larissa together. I've talked to them both and have learned that Russ and Larissa are deliriously happy, despite their differences.

What keeps them coiled in the holy headlock of wedlock? Some might say love. I think there's more to it. I think it's their affection for Vietnamese food. When your biggest problems concern dried porridge and extension cords, an order of pan-fried shrimp rice noodle can mend a lot of fences.

January 17, 1998

It's a mistake to skirt female etiquette

Some questions were invented by men. "Can you hold this transmission on your chest while I find the hoist?" is a question most likely invented by a man.

Same for: "Would you mind bailing out the boat while I get the flare gun?" And: "Can you chop this log in half faster than I can?" And: "Can you reach into my pack and find my first-aid kit? I should keep this arm elevated."

Some questions were invented by women. "Would you mind holding my purse?" (Of course he wouldn't. Are you kidding me?) And: "Did you remember the —." (It doesn't matter what the "—" is. It could be anything from "vanilla extract" to "baby." But while we're on the topic, the answer is no. He didn't remember it.) And especially this question: "What should I bring?" The question, "What should I bring?" has all the earmarks of a female-conceived question. It sounds conciliatory. It sounds open and round and inviting.

"What should I bring?" It's the question she asks when someone has invited them over for dinner. It is automatic, reflexive.

And it's a good thing she answered the phone because if he had, he wouldn't have asked it. After the part where they invite you over, he would have said, "Sounds great, thanks!" and then hung up the phone.

He would have made two mistakes here. First, he would have accepted the invitation without checking with her. "I can't believe you said yes. You didn't even check with me."

"God, sorry. Are we doing something Saturday?"

"No. But that's not the point."

We'll let these two finish their chat and go on to the second mistake. Remember, he's already hung up.

"What should we bring?" she says to him.

"Nothing."

"Did you ask?"

"No."

"Call back." He doesn't want to call back. It would be contrived. And they would know it wasn't really him asking, so it would feel demeaning. "Do I have to?"

"Give me the phone. Sheesh."

Do you think I'm making this up? I've done real-world research. A few months ago, I decided to throw a lunchtime Grey Cup wiener roast for my co-workers. Every male I invited said, "Cool." Every female said, "What should I bring?" Every single one.

And every time one of them asked, it caught me off guard. I didn't want them to bring anything. I didn't think they should have to. So when they said, "What should I bring?" I would say, "Nothing."

Did that satisfy them? Were they happy just to show up? Not a chance. They wouldn't take "nothing" for an answer. "Are you sure?" they would say. It's like they didn't believe me. And then they'd start suggesting things.

"Buns?"

"No, I'm getting buns."

"Drinks?"

"No, I'll have drinks." (Mental note: buy drinks.) They were confounded. They had to bring something. They wouldn't feel good about it otherwise. I'm guessing they would rather not go than go empty-handed.

And I wasn't playing along. I was denying them the opportunity to con-tribute to my event. How selfish of me! Without even knowing it, I was having a hand fight with the female code of conduct. "What should I bring?" a woman would say.

"Nothing."

"How about ketchup and mustard?"

"OK. Ketchup and mustard."

They were wearing me down. I was forced to start giving up hard-earned ground. They sensed my weakness and pressed on. "And relish? Somebody might want relish."

Of course, now that I've had a chance to think about it, I realize that four little words would have saved me a world of trouble. There is an answer to the question, "What should I bring?" That answer is another question: "How about a salad?" That's it. That's all it would have taken to skirt the controversy.

"What should I bring?"

"HOW ABOUT A SALAD?"

"Perfect! I've got this great recipe for blah, blah, blah."

And they leave happy. But I didn't know that yet. Instead, I was still on the defensive. This was supposed to be nice and easy: wieners and buns. And,

OK, drinks. Simple, manageable. Naturally, when I got home, I complained to my wife about my little barbecue spinning out of control with all the unsolicited advice and offers of help. I was on the verge of losing all control over my own event.

"What are you bringing for dessert?" she said.

Feb. 2, 2014

The clothes doth oft proclaim her man

The man had to attend a formal affair, and he was rushing to get out the door.

He wasn't worried about being late, he was hurrying because he knew that if she got home before he left she would make him wear something else. He didn't want to go through that. The humiliation wasn't so bad. It was knowing she would be right. That, and having to wear the proof all night long – the poly-cotton I-told-you-so.

Besides, he was perfectly capable of dressing himself. The results might not be perfect but they would be good enough. What's wrong with good enough?

He decided on the pants first. They looked clean and they didn't need ironing and he hadn't worn them in a while. Dockers. Not messy cargo-ish Dockers but dressy office-ish Dockers. Green but not too green. That's where the outfit would start, he decided. It felt right.

And the best thing: she wasn't home to ask, "Are you going to wear that?"

"Are you going to wear that?" does not mean "Are you going to wear that?" It never has and it never will. What it means is "Don't wear that." But she doesn't want to say "Don't wear that" because she doesn't want to sound shrewish. It's in her nature to seek a consensus. A consensus is when the two of you work together to come to her way of thinking. The trouble is that the one thing she hates more than sounding shrewish is seeing you leave the house wearing what you're wearing.

In other words, "Don't wear those (brown) shoes with that (black) belt."

To him, it's overthinking the situation. The shoes, in and of themselves, are excellent shoes. And the belt, in and of itself, is an excellent belt. They match, you see, because they're both excellent. He's thinking on a higher plane.

In time, if he's lucky, the man will come to understand how the woman thinks. For instance, when you're getting dressed up for a formal event and she's looking awesome, don't make the mistake of thinking that she's done it for you. As far as you're concerned she'd look awesome in anything. This isn't you being flattering, it's you having no standards. She's not going to waste rib-eye steak on a starving Doberman. No, fellas. She's fretted and fussed over the hairdo, the makeup, the dress, the shoes and the purse because she wants to look awesome for other women. It's their opinion that matters. "You mean I'm not in the equation?" you sniff. Friend, you're not even on the chalkboard.

And so the man picked the pants and was about to decide on a shirt when the phone rang. It was her.

"What are you going to wear?" she asked. Translation: "I heard on the radio that it's really fancy, and I'd be mortified if you ended up wearing jeans."

He clenched. She didn't think he was stupid enough to wear jeans, did she?

"I will be suitably attired," he said. It was too evasive. He had barely cleared the trench and he was already giving up ground. But it was worth it. He liked the use of the word "suitably" in reference to dressing. It was pleasing to the palate. He savoured it like good port.

They went back and forth a bit before she said goodbye, sounding not the least bit reassured.

He was in business. Now for a jacket. He was sick, sick, sick of the hound-stooth. He liked the idea of the black blazer. He hadn't worn it in a while. That's a good way to choose clothes – wearing stuff you forgot you had gives you an emotional stake in the outfit. He picked the black shirt for the opposite reason. He wore it a lot because he liked it so much. It looked great (in and of itself). Home stretch. Black shoes, black belt (hey honey, they match!). He was off.

Then the door opened. She was home. She does this thing without even realizing it. It's her own two-second version of the fashion faux-pas TV show *What Not to Wear*. In the first second, she appraises his outfit and mentally lists its shortcomings. In the next second she undergoes an excruciating inner battle: "Should I say something or should I let it go? He'll get mad if I mention it but . . . oh, I just have to." This ends with the sigh. Don't misinterpret the sigh. She's not mad at you. It's not exasperation. It's the sigh of having to do something one doesn't want to do. (Combined with a bit of "I shouldn't even have to tell him this.") Don't take it personally. It's like a plumber sighing before unplugging a toilet.

And so, the other shoe dropped before he had a chance to put it on.

"Is that what you're wearing?"

Since he had his coat in one hand and the car keys in the other it was safe to assume that, yes, the clothes he had on were the clothes he was wearing.

Her worst fears were confirmed. She never liked the black blazer. He tried to wear it with black pants once. That's how he learned that you can't wear black with black because no two blacks are alike. This was a mystery to him on a par with quantum physics. He knew he was cornered on the jacket. The hill he chose to die on was the shirt. The shirt must stay. (In truth, he didn't really care. He just wanted to save something – anything – from the original outfit).

She suggested the tan pants. Fine. She left him alone for a bit. Since the pants were now tan he switched to brown shoes and, like a good boy, the brown belt. She came back. Oh, no, the black belt "sets it off." He didn't know how a belt could set anything off but he was running late now, and it didn't matter. The brown belt came off. The black belt went back on. The brown shoes came off. The black shoes went back on. That left the jacket. Not the houndstooth! Not the houndstooth!

"How about the houndstooth?" she said.

February 9, 2008

Confessions of a Monday night band widower

It has to happen eventually.

You're married for a couple of years. You've settled into a comfortable routine. Then your spouse starts coming home late. She buys black-and-white clothes but never wears them when you're around. When you ask her why she's out until 10 o'clock on Monday nights, she's evasive. Then one day, you're vacuuming the trunk of her car, and you see it: a small black suitcase. You open it with trembling hands. The roar of the vacuum becomes a distant hum and the trunk swims before you as you peer at the contents. In a minute that seems like forever, your deepest fears are confirmed: It's a clarinet all right. A LeBlanc Vito B-flat clarinet. Damn the woodwinds.

There's no doubt about it now. She's joined a band.

It was all so sudden. You knew she played clarinet in high school, but she quit before you met her, and it never seemed real. She didn't talk about it, and you didn't ask. You didn't need to know about those long bus rides to music competitions in Moose Jaw, about the mass camp-outs on strange gym floors. About broken reeds and spit rags and wobbly music stands. Or maybe, just maybe, *she didn't want you to know.*

Ten years later, the old urge flares up. She sees an ad for the adult community band. Just like that, she joins. She even brings home the list of rules and dress code: white shirt, long black skirt or pants, sensible black shoes. It's a little flashy, a little "Vegas" for your tastes, but you keep your mouth shut. There's talk of a spring trip to Calgary. Can the sale of chocolate-covered almonds be far behind?

Soon the practices start. One every week for two, sometimes two-and-a-half hours. You try to develop other interests while she's away. You do the dishes – you even clean the gribblies from the drain thingy, hoping she'll notice. You play the stereo loud, but the house still seems empty. In a desperate moment of weakness, you even glance at the ironing.

It doesn't take long before she's practising in the house, right under your nose. The clarinet goes *doodle, doodle, doodle det.* You turn the TV louder to show it doesn't bother you. Mistake #1.

You try to patch things up by showing interest. "When are you going to play a whole song instead of just scales?" you ask, politely. Mistake #2.

"This *is* a whole song. It's just *my* part of it," she says.

Later, in order to sound "hip," you try to use band slang. "Gonna play your axe tonight, dear?"

"An axe is a guitar. This is a clarinet." There is no slang word for clarinet.

Then you try bragging about her – you tell someone she's joined an orchestra. Strike #3, dummy.

"An orchestra has strings. A band doesn't have strings."

Two months go by. She's mastered *Salvation is Created* by Tschesnokoff. *Aladdin* is a breeze. You hope for some John Philip Sousa – maybe the Monty Python theme song – but dare not ask.

Now it's time for the big Fall Concert. Eager to get a look at the hotshot trombone players and cocky French hornists she's been hanging out with, you can't wait to attend.

The first thing you notice? This band employs no greasy-haired roadies in black T-shirts. Nor does it appear to attract any scantily clad groupies. The question of substance abuse and hotel trashing is not even an issue here. You are relieved.

The second thing you see is the conformity. Ever obedient to their conductor, band members sit down and spring to their feet at the graceful sweep of his hand. Dressed uniformly, the players are a small musical army ready to charge or retreat at the conductor's command. No wonder trains run on time.

The Beginner, Intermediate and Junior bands go first. They do fine, particularly the beginners, who absolutely nail *Long, Long Ago*. A hush falls on the crowd when the Senior band takes its place. There she is, right in the second row where you can see one eye and part of her forehead. She looks up at the conductor a lot, which must be good. You can't hear her play, which is probably a good thing, too. In fact, you can't hear any individual band member play. All those hours at home blowing notes seemingly at random pay off in one smooth wall of sound. The band plays to beat the band.

Overture in B Flat is knocked off without a hitch. The mellifluous *Danny Boy* is no obstacle. And *Star Trek Through the Generations* proves to be a showstopper, particularly since it's played last.

It looks fun. Better than ironing, to be sure. You're slightly jealous. You wonder, briefly, if there's an opening. In the triangle section, maybe?

November 1994

Russ and Larissa go to the dogs

I was shocked to hear that Russ and Larissa had gotten a dog. After all, Russ didn't much like dogs. *Urinatus Territorialis*, he called them.

Dogs are time-consuming animals that require regular feeding and frequent exercise. From what I'd heard, Russ had his hands full providing precisely those necessities to his boys.

"Don't they wreck the furniture if they get bored?" I asked Russ over lunch the other day.

"Yeah, but if you let them watch *Toy Story* they settle right down," he said.

Eventually, Russ admitted that it wasn't his idea to get a dog. His kids had wanted one since they were old enough to pronounce the word. In fact, they were dog crazy. They could spot a canine from three blocks away. The sighting, always accompanied by the ear-splitting shriek of "PUPPY!" commanded the owner to heel and let the children pet the pet.

"Then the nagging started," Russ sighed, sniffing the menu.

Apparently, this was not the mild, strategic pestering that an older child or teenager might employ: catching their parents in a good mood, offering reasonable explanations for what they so desperately want – the careful deployment of high-tech smart-nags, one might say. No, this was good old-fashioned carpet nagging.

"When can we get a puppy?"

"When can we get a puppy?"

"When can we get a puppy?"

It continued every hour of every day until our stubborn resolve eventually wilted into acquiescence.

Larissa broke down first. In fact, she began to like the idea. In fact, she started dog shopping. According to the books, a small, non-shedding, dumb dog is the easiest to live with. Then Larissa saw Jake smiling at her from his cell on death row. Jake was a big, lustily shedding, highly intellectual dog. Part border collie, in fact. Border collies are brilliant, the experts say. When no one's around, they match all the colours on Rubik's cubes. Then they eat them.

So it was that on a warm, late-summer day, Jake cheated death and hit the jackpot: two walks per day, regular bowls full of not-the-least-expensive dog food, the fanatical attention of two boys who think a dog is a toy that never needs new batteries.

"It's bliss," Russ said, licking his soup bowl.

"Oh yeah? What about the expense? What about the smell?" I wondered.

"Or the layer of fur on the kitchen floor at the end of every day? Or all the new stains on the carpet? Or the endless walking? Or the kids practising animal research on the thing? It's bliss," Russ insisted.

I had my doubts.

"What about cleaning up all the you-know-what?" (I know Russ to be squeamish; I've seen him gag at the sight of moldy bread.) How was the poop getting scooped? Gingerly, as it turned out.

"The first time I had to clean it up, I couldn't decide which was more disgusting – letting it get cold first or bagging it while it was still hot," Russ admitted. Now, he just turns his head and coughs.

It took a while for "Jakey-boy," as he's often called, to get used to his new family. They could tell he was feeling more at home the day he pulled one of the seat cushions off the couch when everyone was away, unzipped it and chewed the foam into bits.

The books say it's unproductive to scold a dog for doing something like this. It's better to "redirect" its behaviour, which is why Larissa gave Jake some rawhide to chew on when they were away. When they got back, dirt was strewn all over the floor; the dog had dug a hole in the plant to hide his rawhide.

In the ensuing weeks, Jake chewed:
- a nice pair of all-terrain shoes
- an intercontinental ballistic missile from a toy army set
- the skin off a baseball (digesting everything but the red strings)

"He also has a weakness for the glue used to bind books," said Russ. "One day, he ate our copy of *101 Dalmatians*."

"How apt," I offered.

Things got downright ugly a while later when a hunter friend of Russ's donated some lovely looking moose bones. Jake spent hours gnawing on the succulent fibula. In the ensuing 24 hours, Jake:
- threw up under the dining room table
- voided on the carpet at the top of the stairs
- begged to be let outside to relieve himself at 2 a.m., 4 a.m. and 6 a.m.
- had a diarrhea event on the living room carpet

"We've spent more on carpet cleaner in the last three months than the Centennial Auditorium," Russ howled.

"I'm sensing a little resentment, fella," I told him.

"Oh no, I'm fine. He's a cute dog, and I'm getting used to him," Russ said, scratching himself behind the ear.

Lunch was over. I reached for the bill. Russ thought I was trying to steal one of his fries. He growled and bit my hand.

"Nice boy," I said, backing out of the restaurant.

December 1, 2001

Larissa teaches Russ how to mince

Russ and Larissa are awesome apart. When she's away for the weekend, Russ shines. He plans fun things to do. He orders Chinese food. He packs the fridge with caffeine-free Diet Pepsi for the kids and, for himself, a load of beer that would crush a mule. The weekend flies by.

And when Russ gets home from a few days away, the kids are bursting to tell him all the fun they had with their mom. They went to *Iron Man*. They saw the new tigers at the zoo. Two happy kids plus a mother or a father. That's family togetherness at its best.

Russ and Larissa are pretty great during the workday, too. They send quick emails back and forth arranging which one of them will go home for lunch and who will pick up whichever kid needs picking up. They share important news.

"Jim Cuddy – September 27!"

"I know. Just heard."

It's an efficient, affable relationship. It's only when they're together that things sometimes go off the rails. And usually, it has something to do with household chores. Russ is informally banned from touching laundry, for instance. The aftershocks of the Great Shrunken Bra Scandal of '98 are still being felt. This has turned Russ into a secret laundry doer. If Larissa's away for a day, he's been known to wash a load or two. What a rebel. When laundry is outlawed, only outlaws do laundry. Sometimes, with malice aforethought, he'll even throw a tea towel in with the underwear. What's detergent for, after all?

He's failed to earn trust on the vacuuming front as well.

"Did you use the wand and get the edge of the baseboard?"

"Of course!"

She has to ask? What an insult. What kind of vacuumer does she think he is?

"No, you didn't – look at the dog hair."

Busted. But it's in the kitchen where togetherness isn't necessarily all it's cracked up to be. If you want to make an omelette, you have to break a few eggs. If you want worlds to collide, try cracking Mars against Venus.

Russ is what you might call an intuitive cook. He doesn't like measuring. He eschews recipes in favour of things he just thinks might go well together. The other day, he made a sort of quiche with Bisquick mix, eggs and sausage. Sounded good in theory. In practice, the dough tripled in size, dwarfing the toppings, which were half-gone by the time the first serving was served. There were plenty of leftovers – never a good sign – and they had been quietly made to disappear when Russ's back was turned.

Larissa likes recipes. They're tried and trusted. They lend a certain credibility to a meal. When Larissa is cooking, there are lots of measuring cups and spoons to wash. She actually likes measuring. What she doesn't like are large bits of food in her food. If you want your hamburger scramble-fried, let her do it. Each particle of ground meat will be separate and distinct from the other. It takes skill to do this properly. It also takes about an hour and a half. Russ doesn't have that much patience. He's been known to sneak the burner up from low to medium-high just to get things moving. His scramble-fried hamburger comes out in about four chunks per pound.

Russ and Larissa agree on many things. Her popcorn is an art form. He makes a great Caesar salad. But when the knives come out, they've had some strained conversations about the difference between "chopped" and "minced." Russ was influenced early by the TV chefs Emeril Lagasse and the late James Barber. Their idea of chopping an onion was waving a knife somewhere in its vicinity. This "rustic" cooking method appeals to Russ. He pictures himself in a 19th-century farmhouse in Tuscany with tables made of timbers as thick as your leg and a whole pig roasting on a spit. In these environs, a rough-hewn onion tells everyone what kind of person you are – casual, rugged, individualistic.

Not so Larissa, who sees some sort of divine order in a cutting board paved with identical specks of onion. Russ likes chopped onions. Larissa likes minced. But this is a marriage so they compromise and go with minced.

Their tastes in food differ as well. Russ is a meaty boy. Nothing's better to him than a slab of roasted flesh surrounded by some mashed potatoes and frozen peas. Larissa is all about pasta and a creamy sauce. If the recipe ends with the words "until hot and bubbly," she's all for it. This leads inevitably to casseroles. Casseroles make Russ want to cry. Once you mix the ingredients, why don't you just warm them up in the microwave and start eating? What possible difference could 350 degrees for 40 minutes make? He's hungry now.

It has taken awhile, but the two have learned that there is a time in a marriage for ribs and a time for tuna melts. Putting your partner's need for spinach and phyllo before your own need for brisket, seasoned with a dry rub and slow-roasted for half a day until it melts in your mouth, is the key to domestic bliss. Russ understands this, just as Larissa knows that when Russ comes home from the store with crushed pineapple instead of chunked, it's merely a sign that he's not that bright – not that he doesn't love her. The right ingredients, evenly matched, each serving the other; these are the keys to domestic bliss.

And things can only get better now that Russ and Larissa are renovating their kitchen. She likes one-handle faucets. He likes two-handle faucets. They're going to compromise.

September 13, 2008

A simple brake light isn't going to stop Russ

Why did he do it? Why did Russ end up breaking the bulb socket when his wife told him to be careful?

The reason is as deep and complex as Man himself. So deep, and so complex, that Man himself doesn't have a smidge of a clue why. Not a smidge. He is, after all, just a man.

It started with a burned-out brake light bulb on the used car that Russ and Larissa had just purchased. It was the only thing wrong with the vehicle. They didn't notice it until they drove the car home. To Russ, it was a problem that merited – nay, demanded – swift and decisive action. Their used car didn't seem new with such a (non-) glaring flaw.

Being a man, Russ knew how simple it was to change an automotive light bulb. As long as it's not a headlight bulb. Headlight bulbs are tricky because you have to wedge your hand into a tiny space and turn a socket without bending your fingers. It's like trying to pick a dime off the floor behind a clothes dryer. It's one degree short of impossible. You strain, you reach, you cramp what needs to be cramped, but you get the job done.

In contrast, the light bulb that Russ had to deal with was easy-peasy, a mere speed bump in the parking lot below Mount Everest. It was the "centre high-mounted stop lamp." Introduced in 1986, the "centre high-mounted stop lamp" is surely one of the most specifically named of all auto parts. The "centre high-mounted stop lamp" is mounted high, in the centre, of the back of your vehicle. If you were phoning an auto-parts store, the conversation would go something like this:

"Hi. I need a bulb for a centre high-mounted stop lamp."

"The one in the middle?"

"Yes."

"Mounted up high?"

"Yes."

"On the back of the vehicle?"

"Yes."

"And it's a stop lamp?"

"Yes."

"Just a minute, I'll have to check."

The centre high-mounted stop lamp on Russ and Larissa's new used car was located behind a plastic lens. There were two screws holding the lens in place. Clearly, Russ told me later, it was simply a matter of unscrewing the two screws, removing the lens, twisting the bulb out and putting in a new one. Russ even had the right kind of replacement bulb in the Surplus Auto Bulb Department of his garage, he thought, so there was no point in delaying the procedure whatsoever.

What would constitute a delay? Reading the instructions in the owner's manual. Verifying the procedure on an auto website. Taking a deep breath first. In other words, everything that Larissa thought would be prudent. "Are you sure that's how it comes off?" Larissa asked Russ as he hurried back from the garage with a screwdriver.

This is the difference between men and women. A man seeks knowledge by experience. A man doesn't know if "that's how it comes off." He won't know if "that's how it comes off" until he tries. So he has to try. Right. This. Second.

In this case, Russ's knowledge suddenly began to expand when he found out the lens was held down by sticky caulking. Essentially, it was glued to the car. Clearly, he would argue, the first thing to do was peel the lens away from the sticky caulking. He poked and grunted and started to sweat, which attracted a cloud of mosquitos. The sun had set, so there was a time element involved as well. A two-minute job had suddenly become A Project.

"Are you sure you know what you're doing?" Larissa asked.

The truthful answer would be "no." But to a man, "no" is no reason to stop. In fact, it's the best reason there is to press on. Quitting won't fix the problem.

Larissa, apparently, was less than impressed with this logic when Russ took a flat-bladed screwdriver to the back of their new used car and started to poke and pry. She could barely stand to look at all when Russ got the lens off and started to yank on the bulb housing. To him, this was progress. To her, he was living on borrowed time.

Long story short: the housing was stuck, Russ forced it too much and ended up breaking the bulb socket. That's when Russ realized that the bulb is actually accessible from the inside of the vehicle, not the outside. He'd have to buy a new socket.

Russ's knowledge base had expanded exponentially. This, to him, was a good thing. To Larissa, it was more like, "we've owned this car for 10 minutes and now there's something broken on it."

Technically, that wasn't true, since the car already had a broken light bulb. Russ could easily have pointed this fact out to Larissa but he chose not to – something about discretion being the better part of valour.

So did Russ screw up? Or did he gain valuable, real-world experience in the field of centre high-mounted stop lamps? Isn't the answer obvious?

In summary, you can't put a price on a lesson like this – if you don't count the fact that a new bulb socket costs $26.35. Don't mention this to Larissa. She wouldn't understand.

August 5, 2012

Russ and Larissa buy a book

In male-female relations, Russ has evolved. First, he thought he understood women. Surely they were just like men, but with more interesting standard equipment.

But that assumption was challenged when he read an article that claimed women like to express their feelings by saying things. That explained a lot, like why Larissa was talking while he was clearly reading a car magazine. Russ didn't need to talk to express himself. He could express his feelings by doing things like driving fast or watching NASCAR. It worked whether he was happy or unhappy.

The realization that women needed to have conversations settled upon him with the heavy weight of obligation. He could converse. He would converse. It was just too bad he had to converse.

The next step in his progress was realizing that he didn't understand women, but would – in time. But years went by without Russ learning how one colour of paint could be better than another – WHEN THEY WERE IDENTICAL.

Finally, it dawned on Russ that he didn't understand women and never would. Yes, he'd fallen short of his youthful ambitions, but the workload was greatly reduced.

That state of blissful ignorance came in handy the other day when it was time to give a gift to a new baby in the family. Russ knew he was out of his league. There was no point suggesting what to buy ("A drone! They're super-cool and she'll grow into it!") or where they should buy it or when or how it would be wrapped or if it should come with a card. ("A card? Why are we wasting money on a card?")

Did he agree that a book was the best thing to give? Of course he did. And the book would come from the city's finest bookstore, a place so large, so book-filled that it had its own restaurant to feed people who would be missing meals from all that book-looking.

As it happened, there were not one but three new babies in the family, which made shopping exponentially more complicated. For Larissa, that is. Russ could have found three books and been out of there before his car's muffler starting making that tic-tic-tic cooling down noise.

Did you know the word "patience" comes from the Latin word for "pain?" What transpired, as Russ patiently looked on, was a balancing act that would have made the Wallenda family blush. Larissa painstakingly started to choose, not the books themselves, but candidates. She was compiling what appeared to be a longlist – which would be pared down to a shortlist – before the final round of selections. Each column of books would fit within certain thematic parameters, the prices of each being consistent among the three columns.

There was an algorithm going on here that Russ would never fathom, and he knew it. He also knew it would be folly to jump in and start suggesting titles.

His input not strictly speaking (or unstrictly speaking) required, Russ strayed one row over and saw a collection of books with titles like *Joint Custody with a Jerk* and *We Have Two Homes Now*. The divorce section! It faced the Dr. Seuss section. Green Eggs and Alimony.

Unnerved by the divorce section, Russ retreated to a child-sized stool in the reading circle and waited for nature to take its course. Gradually, and with great consideration given to the pros and cons of each literary gem, the shortlist was winnowed down to the actual books that would be purchased. To the till!

Was the errand finished at that point? Even Russ knew it wasn't. Each set of books would have to go into something, and that something was a gift bag. To the dollar store!

Russ dropped Larissa off and took his time parking. When he rejoined her, she was matching the colour of tissue paper to the gift bags. The young Russ would have been like, "Are you kidding? Who cares?" But by now, he'd learned that it did matter. It mattered a lot. He didn't know how it mattered a lot, but that was not the point.

Even so, something about the tissue paper got to him and Russ made an involuntary noise like a magpie interrupted. That half-squawk of dissension instantly betrayed his incredulity. ("Oh, come on, it's only tissue paper!") Russ could only hope that Larissa hadn't heard. He didn't want to be seen as less "into" the shopping trip than she was. He really didn't. In fact, not shopping took at least as much effort as shopping and, in his mind at least, Russ had just put in a gruelling shift.

If he were better at expressing his feelings, Russ would have communicated all that to Larissa when they got home. But he wasn't. And besides, NASCAR was on and there were only 64 laps left. If there was anything more exciting than gift bag tissue paper, it was cars going around in a circle.

March 29, 2015

When Russ and Larissa's driving styles collide

They don't argue that much. At least, that's what they tell me. But if anything can transform the finely tuned machine of Russ and Larissa's marriage into a smoking, clunking hunk of junk, it's driving.

It's not a matter of who's the better driver. It's more a question of who's the worst passenger. Russ isn't great, I can tell you. He's got this habit of driving vicariously from the right-hand seat. If something seems to be going wrong, he'll tense up, brace his hands on the dash and slam on an imaginary brake pedal.

Not his fault, Russ claims. He says he inherited the trait from his father, an imaginary-brake-pedal-presser from way back. That's pretty much how Russ learned to drive. He'd be sailing through an uncontrolled intersection, protected only by a learner's permit and 3,500 pounds of Dodge Monaco, and his dad would hit the brake-pedal-that-wasn't-there and glare at him as if he'd just aimed at a row of toddling ducklings.

"What if somebody was coming?" he'd yell.

"Well, then I'd stop. And no one was," Russ would say. And then the lecture would begin.

If only to placate his father, Russ began to slow down at uncontrolled intersections, even if he had the right of way. After avoiding a close call or two, he came to realize that the old man was right. Russ went on to get his driver's licence (on the first try) and became one of the best drivers he knows. According to him, anyway.

Therefore, it always offends Russ when Larissa questions his driving; he can't quite believe it – it's like someone finding fault with the Hope Diamond or something.

"You're going too fast," she will say.

"But everybody speeds here," he'll counter.

It doesn't help matters that Larissa gets an instant headache when he turns the wheel abruptly. He'll look over and she'll have her head back and her eyes closed – like a martyr finding inner strength while being subjected to unspeakable torture.

"You're like the Princess and the Pea of passengers," he said to her once. That did not go over well.

They can't even agree on parking. She'll go underground at the grocery store every time. "Smells like rancid muffins down there," he says.

And at the mall, he doesn't mind walking a little. She will circle, shopping for the closest available space.

They even disagree on when NOT to drive. Or they used to. When they lived downtown, Russ insisted on walking to the office formal one December. He didn't take into account the wind. By the time they got to the hotel, Larissa's up-do was more of a side-do. It was not a Merry Christmas.

But most recently, it was that genetic panic reflex that got Russ in trouble. Larissa (who got her licence on the first try) was behind the wheel when it happened.

"She was going too fast," Russ contends. "And there was this row of cars stopped in front of us. The road was icy, and she was going to pile right into them."

He did what he always does: tensed up, sucked in a quick, loud, hissing breath through his teeth – the same noise you'd make before jumping off a dock into an ice-cold lake – and slammed his right foot into the floor.

Her reaction was as immediate as someone who's been snuck up on and had "BOO!" yelled in her ear. Larissa involuntarily hit the actual brake pedal. Then she realized she was reacting to Russ's overreaction. Her response was less than appreciative. Not, "Thanks for the warning, honey." More like, "Why do you DO that?" And the argument revved up.

First gear: "Because you were going too fast."

"No, I wasn't!"

Second gear: "And it was icy."

"No, it wasn't!"

Third gear: "And those cars were stopped right in front of us."

"They were moving. And THEY WERE HALF A BLOCK AWAY!"

There are two sides to every car and, clearly, two sides to every story.

Thus was a pleasant car ride ruined by a crazed suburban mom hell-bent on turning the peaceful city streets into Carmageddon OR an alert passenger politely offering some prudent advice (depending on whom you believe).

You could have cut the tension with the Jaws of Life. Or maybe not.

"Fine then," she said.

"Fine then," he said.

Silence followed. Russ had made his point, he believed, and had nothing more to offer. But Larissa did.

"It's like that time at Waskesiu," she finally said.

It was a stab in the heart. Russ knew exactly what she was talking about, even though the incident had occurred some 20 years before. When you're leaving the famous resort, there's a fork in the road. Larissa, who was driving, went straight. Russ instantly realized she was going the wrong way. He screamed, "Stop!" and did that imaginary braking thing. Not used to his antics that early in their relationship, Larissa floored her brake pedal, locking all four wheels until the car came to rest on the fresh blacktop.

That's when Russ realized he was wrong. And – worse – each front tire had a flat spot from being locked from 100 kilometres an hour to zero.

So on this night, two decades later, he had to reluctantly admit he was a habitual overreactor.

"You're right," he said.

Then she said something else.

"You're right," he said again.

And then she made her next point.

"You're right," he said. It was the opposite of arguing. But can there be too much agreement in a relationship? Doesn't the marriage machine need compression and spark to keep it running? After the last "You're right," from Russ, Larissa paused.

"This isn't any fun," she said.

"You're right," said Russ.

April 14, 2013

Russ and Larissa rock out with Coldplay

Russ and Larissa recently ventured to the city of Edmonton to attend a concert by the British band Coldplay.

Larissa loves Coldplay. Russ didn't know how much she loved Coldplay until Larissa bought two tickets to Coldplay and booked a posh hotel room for two nights as a birthday present from both of them to herself, but mainly from herself to herself. She presented these facts to Russ as a *fait accompli*, but he was all for it because he could look like a supportive husband without doing a lick of shopping. Win-win.

Russ had nothing against Coldplay, but, to him, Coldplay and Oasis and Radiohead were pretty much the same band. Coldhead? Radioplay? Who? Actually, he did know that Chris Martin was the frontman of Coldplay. When Russ remembered that Chris Martin was once married to Gwyneth Paltrow, he had much more sympathy for Chris Martin.

But still, a trip to the big city with the lovely Larissa was reason enough to like Coldplay for a day or two.

Their hotel had a brand new Lexus SUV out front and a sign that said guests could request a complimentary ride in it. "Complimentary" happened to be one of Russ's favourite words, so instead of walking four blocks to the restaurant, they got the concierge to drive them. The Lexus had a stadium-sized info screen and red leather seats. It was like sitting in a home theatre in a mansion but with pedestrians zipping by.

The hotel had a complimentary breakfast as well. Russ was encouraged to see that Edmonton cuisine was a lot like the food back home, so he filled up on scrambled eggs and sausages.

There was one huge difference, however. Edmonton has an Ikea, an Ikea so big that it has its own gravitational pull. All you have to do is get into your car and Ikea will draw you into itself.

In case you're wondering how middle-aged people kill time before a rock concert, it's by spending several hours comparing one white melamine shelving unit to another white melamine shelving unit. (Don't call Russ a hero, that word is thrown around far too much these days.)

Ikea did not disappoint. They had everything from laundry hampers to beds to chairs to forks to lamps, and they each had a name like Svunk and Jouleg and Bartt and Njord.

The problem is that Russ and Larissa already have a house full of stuff, so a journey through the fjords of Ikea was a bit like going grocery shopping after you've shut down the all-you-can-eat buffet. But they came all that way so they bought something – a white melamine night table named Llarz or some such thing – it's quite possible that Ikea won't let you leave unless you do.

Like Ikea furniture, the set-up for the Coldplay concert would have taken a long time and many, many hexagonal wrenches to assemble. There were three stages and a long runway for Chris Martin to caper upon. Confetti cannons exploded throughout. There were huge balloons for the audience to bat around. The second song was *Yellow*. Russ forgot that *Yellow* was a Coldplay song, which is a good thing because he's always hated *Yellow*.

Twenty thousand people were going crazy for *Yellow* and Russ was thinking, "If this was *Spaceship Superstar* by Prism, I'd be more into it. Now THAT'S a song."

Before the concert, every ticket holder was handed a wristband that lit up in various colours. The curious thing is that Russ's wristband didn't work. It was as if Coldplay knew he wasn't a believer – like the kid in *Polar Express* who can't hear the bell because he doesn't believe in Santa.

But Larissa believed in Coldplay, and she was elated from start to finish. It warmed Russ's heart to see her so happy and her wristband lighting up when it was supposed to.

Larissa left the concert feeling wonderful. She had songs like *Clocks* and *Fix You* going through her head. Russ was content as well.

He was thinking about *Lay It on the Line* by Triumph.

Now THAT'S a song.

September 30, 2017

Chapter 5

The Unqualified Joy of Parenting or The Joy of Unqualified Parenting

I remember the exact second everything changed. It was the third week of July 1996. My wife, eight months pregnant, had been in the hospital for 17 days on bed rest – a precaution because we were having twins. I was taking my bike to work a lot then, a beautiful eight-kilometre ride along the riverbank.

Around noon on July 19, the mother-to-be called me at work. The "to-be" part was about to be removed from her job description. I hopped on my bike and pedalled to the hospital. There were two complete medical teams in place, which was the protocol for twins. I guess they didn't want the second baby to pop out and fly across the room when their backs were turned.

The doctors were supremely confident. In fact, they were almost annoyingly supremely confident. "This isn't a Saturday oil change!" I thought. "How about some furrowed brows, you guys – a little consternation to make us feel special?"

I suited up in the appropriate disposable protective garb. A paper hat's bacteria-blocking power is the key to a successful delivery. After that, there was a lot of sweating, panting and gritting of teeth – some by my wife. And then, the crowning moment: toast and jam back in the room! Yes, it was quite a day.

Oh, yes, there were babies as well. Sometime around 4 p.m., two infant humans squished into our lives like angry prunes. Joseph, the elder by 22 minutes, tipped the scales at five pounds, seven ounces. William, the younger, was five pounds, 15 ounces. Joe was looking a little jaundiced. The nurses whisked him off to the heat lamp for a tropical vacation and, perhaps, umbrella drinks. Other than that complication, it all went great. I found a payphone and called everyone with the news.

"Two boys," I told my father.

"Very good then," he said, and hung up.

No "How much do they weigh?" No "Hair colour?" No "Who do they look like?" No "Do you have names yet?" Pretty much every fact my mother had been waiting months to learn. He caught hell for that, I can tell you.

After the phone calls, some longer than others, the biggest day ever was over. Leaving my exhausted wife, I located my bike and started pedalling home around midnight. Halfway there, it hit me: I was a father. You'd think I would have figured that out by now but, no.

A voice in my head whispered, "Nothing will ever be the same again." A hypothetical fact a day ago was now as indisputable as the rising sun.

It's that moment I remember vividly. In the space of two pedal strokes, I went from a guy to a dad. It's a job for life. Your babies will grow and grow up. But you won't stop being their parent until you stop being. This washed over me in a second, a terrifying and awe-inspiring realization. Maybe it was time to put the toys away.

And so began a journey that would be harder, messier and more complicated than I could ever have imagined. Some days lasted forever. Years went by in a blur. In the background were flannel pajamas, Christmas mornings, first steps, inexplicable tantrums, general cuteness and a fair bit of throw up.

As far as my column went, the wonder, frustration and absurdity of parenting were topics as irresistible as cookies on a high shelf. My kid columns went unchallenged until my twin inspirations were old enough to give me hell for writing about them.

As a writer, all you can hope for is that the reader might identify, take solace, be amused. But, selfishly, my kid columns are also notes to myself – documentary evidence of the hard slogging, lest I get too senti-mental, proof of that awesome innocence, lest I got too discouraged. Maybe this is why humans write. You scratch messages on the cell wall so the next occupant will know you existed. But your children provide the same proof, don't they?

Shooting the breeze on an April Sunday

The neat thing about being a parent is that it gives you a front-row seat on the making of a human being. It's the greatest show on earth, so naturally the tickets are really expensive. They cost a nice chunk of your income, most of your energy and a lot of your youth, as a matter of fact.

But what a great view you get in return. An unimaginably complicated lifetime of events lies ahead for your child, but in the first few months there is relative simplicity. You can pinpoint the exact time and date when every major event transpires in his life: the day he rolls over for the first time, the first time he sits up, his first tooth, his first crawl into the kitchen. The future may be frighteningly unpredictable, but in the present there is order and precision. I can tell you, for instance, the precise moment when the wind tousled my little William's hair for the first time. It was last Sunday, April 13, about 5:30 in the afternoon. He and his brother Joseph are nine months old today, which is only slightly older than the winter, which stopped tormenting us last week. Before winter hit, Will and Joe didn't have much hair to blow around, and they were rarely outside. After the cold came, we never took them out without a tuque or hood or both. If there was any wind around, they certainly weren't aware of it. The change of seasons has opened up a new world to these kids and their parents.

Last Sunday, I took the boys out for a stroller ride. For the first time this year, we left the detestable snowsuits at home. (I'm considering holding a ritual snowsuit burning to celebrate the end of the cold.) I felt like a bear emerging from a cave after hibernation. I wanted to introduce my cubs to the world – or as much of the world as they could see underneath the hoods of their new spring jackets. They were so intrigued they fell asleep within half a block. Ah, but there was fun when we got home. Will woke up first, so I plucked him out of the stroller, pulled his hood down and introduced him to the yard he's never been in before. We saw the grass, we saw the apple tree, we saw the garden and looked at all the dirt he and Joe would be wearing and eating in a few weeks. He saw my bike for the first time, the one I rode home from the hospital on the day he was born; the one I used to ride all the time before parenthood turned me into a rushed and peevish motorist again.

At the end of the tour, Will looked at the kids across the street jumping on a trampoline. He's never seen them before. Then the wind came up and blew his hair around. He squinted into the breeze and smiled as if it tickled his face. That's it. That's all that happened. It was one tiny, insignificant event in a lifetime that's just standing on the threshold. But the wind hit me too, and it caught me off guard. Here's my son, the picture of innocence and trust, letting the wind touch his face. And on this day, the fates have decided to reward his faith with a soft spring breeze that makes him smile. I approve. But there's a catch. There's always a catch. I don't want him to feel any other kind of wind, you see. This little human thinks there is nothing bad in the world. I know he's wrong, but he's going to have to find that out for himself. He's never fallen off a bike. He's never been pushed around by big kids. He's never been yelled at. He's never been cold or afraid. Judging by how often he eats, he's never been hungry, either. So what happens when the winds shift?

I wonder how my guys will react when the breeze bites instead of caresses. When the wind doubles them over and freezes the tears on their cheeks, will they fight their way through it or follow the weak in retreat? Where will they get the strength? Everything is countless and finite at the same time. I wonder how many times my boys will look into a fresh spring breeze and smile. How many Aprils will they be given? Which one gets less and why? My instinct is to protect these little men from every harsh gust that will come their way – every skinned knee, every schoolyard bully, every speck of evil in this big, unpredictable world. But I am as powerless to do that as I am to predict the direction and intensity of tomorrow's breeze.

I can't stop the wind, but I can't stop thinking about it, either.

April 19, 1997

Happy birthday to us . . . we deserve it

July 19 probably has no special significance for you but it does for me. July 19 is my kids' birthday. They are one year old today.

July 19 is also the date I became a father and changed from a selfish, immature person to a tired, selfish, immature person. It's also the date that I began an intensive research project on the risks and rewards of raising young humans. I can sum up my findings in one sentence:

"Kids: you can't live with 'em, they can't live without you."

Let's be clear on one thing, I was a good complainer before I had kids. Now, I'm world class. If I'm twice as good at whining as other new parents, it's probably because we have twins. The good thing about twins is that they have the same birthday. That means one party, one cake and one set of dishes to do. I like that idea.

But aren't first birthdays a little forced? The kids don't know what's going on. They won't remember it. It's a photo opportunity with dessert. At least, that's what I thought as a non-parent. As a parent, I now realize that the first birthday is a day to celebrate the fact that the parents survived the first 365 days. Happy birthday to us.

I'd like to tell you this was the hardest year of my life. I'd like to claim fatherhood has, at times, brought out the worst in me. In fact, I think I will. But first, a few thank yous.

Thank you to my brother-in-law who, upon learning we were expecting, said, "Say goodbye to the rest of your hair."

Thank you to the good folks at Similac for insisting that unused portions of baby formula be poured down the drain. I declare July 19 to be Formula Freedom Day – the day I've poured as much liquid gold down the sink as the babies have actually consumed. At $7 a can, that works out to about $1,200.

Thank you to the Mammary Mafia for making us feel guilty for using formula.

Thank you to all those seasoned parents out there for their loving advice – specifically, those who assured us (after we survived a month of not sleeping for more than three hours in a row) that "it doesn't get any easier."

Has parenthood changed me? Well, I swore I'd never talk baby talk. Luckily, I don't. The sentence "Come here, you cutie scootie wootie lootie tootie" just happens to make perfect sense to me.

And now, a word on shelving. You know, I used to be one of those garage project guys. I'd paint and build and fix stuff to my heart's content out there. Last June, I was building two small pine shelves for the kids' room when one of the electrical sockets in the garage fritzed out. I finished the shelves with my usual efficiency and dedication, however. Will and Joe were born a month later. As of this moment, not only are the shelves not installed (a 20-minute job) but the electrical socket in the garage is still not fixed. I've got a calendar on the same garage wall. It literally never saw April; it was May before I had time to turn the page from March.

It's not that there isn't any free time. Actually, there's plenty. The trouble is that it falls between 10 p.m. and 6 a.m. If I were an owl, I'd get a lot done. Instead, I'm just owly.

The truth is, I have absolutely nothing to complain about. Our yearlings are healthy, happy and good. They never got colic. They've had exactly three colds in their lives. We are getting through teething relatively unscathed, and the boys are not hanging around with any unsavoury neighbourhood babies. But, you know what? I think I'll complain anyway. Hey, it's my party, and I'll gripe if I want to. You would gripe too if twins happened to you.

I would like to state now, for the first time publicly, that I have no sympathy for people who think one infant is a lot of work. It isn't. Try twice the bathing, twice the diapering, twice the rocking to sleep. Try comforting two caterwauling infants at the same time. You can't. I fondly recall the night Baby B woke up crying. I rocked him back to sleep, but not before he woke up Baby A, who then woke up Baby B. Meet the Brothers Grim.

What I really love are the 13-months-apart moms. You know who they are. "I can imagine what twins are like because we had two in 13 months!" they tell us. This is their badge of honour: a kid who can walk and feed himself before the second one arrives. Two in 13 months? Sorry, lady. We had two on the *same day*.

There are harder combinations than two, of course. Having a toddler and twin infants would be worse. So would twin toddlers and a single infant. Or two sets of twins. While we're at it, let's observe a moment of silence for parents of triplets and higher-order multiples. As far as I'm concerned, they are saints if they survive and martyrs if they don't.

It hasn't been all toil, of course. The rewards are small but powerful. Getting happily mauled by two spunky cuties at the end of the day is indescribably wonderful.

In time, I'll forget about laying my clothes out fireman-style at bedtime in preparation for the inevitable night wakings. I'll forget about the day I didn't eat a thing until 8 p.m. even though I had gone home for lunch.

One thing I won't forget is the feeling I had after the first week: "I have worked hard," I thought. "I have given absolutely everything I can. I have earned a break." And then it hit me: I wasn't going to get a break. Ever. You will never not worry about your kids. They will never not be your cuties.

At first, they're a burden. In time, they're a gift. What a difference a year makes. Happy birthday, boys.

July 19, 1997

It's never too late for a green snack

It's 9:55 p.m. Safeway closes at 10. And I'm running – running – across the parking lot.

"What if they lock the door before 10?" I wonder, fighting the panic. I get close to the automatic door. It slides open. Thank God, I'm in. I dash through the vestibule where they park the shopping carts. There's a guy there, impatiently waiting to clean the floors. The sooner I'm out, the sooner he can start and the sooner he'll be done. I avoid eye contact and walk briskly into the store.

Please don't ask to help me. Frankly, I'd be too embarrassed to admit what I'm after. I am going to do this myself. Come hell or high water, I am going to find . . . a green snack.

Tomorrow is Green Day at kindergarten, you see. The kids will wear green clothes. They will learn about things that are green. Perhaps they will rock out to the band Green Day. "Remember to pack a green snack," the note from their teacher said. That was a couple of days ago. Naturally, we procrastinated on the green snack issue until the last minute. Which is why I'm standing in the pudding aisle at Safeway at 10 o'clock on a Wednesday night with my heart pounding and my palms sweating. I'm looking for green Jell-O. Pre-made green Jell-O, to be specific. You see it all the time when you don't need it. When you don't need it, there's so much green Jell-O in the aisles you can hardly push your cart through. Not tonight, however. Tonight, when green Jell-O will solve the problems of the world, what do I find? Orange and raspberry.

"Plan B, Plan B, Plan B," I think. "What's Plan B?" I have no Plan B. I have to find something else that's green and edible. That rules out broccoli. That rules out celery and romaine lettuce and cucumbers. Brussels sprouts? Are you kidding? Do you want the teacher to call Social Services?

The pressure is on. What's green and snack-like? Twizzlers! In the old days, they used to make green Twizzlers. Maybe they still have them. No such luck. Every candy I can find is either red or yellow or blue. There is definite discrimination in the candy world against the colour green.

When it comes down to it, I'm pushing my luck even considering candy. If word gets out that we let our kids eat candy, we'll be branded as irresponsible parents. Ideally, I should be finding a delicious, nutritious, vitamin-laden green snack that's high in fibre, contains no artificial flavours or preservatives and comes in an eco-friendly package. Yeah, I'm screwed.

But failure is not an option. I must find a green snack. If I don't, my kids will be the only ones in the class without one. They'll be humiliated. Their friends will shun them. They will lapse into depression. They'll end up hating school. They'll flunk out. Their lives will be ruined. The penitentiaries of the nation are filled with villains and cut throats whose parents neglected to find them green snacks a month into kindergarten.

I had an uneasy feeling about this kindergarten thing right from the start. On the first day, my kids came home from school with a big, thick envelope in each of their backpacks. Each envelope contained a bunch of papers that I didn't read and a hefty coupon book that could save me, literally, thousands of dollars. How thoughtful! I thought. A welcome-to-school present! It was a day or two before I realized that the books cost $25 each and we were expected to sell as many as we could in order to raise money for the school. Doh!

The question of homework is another vexing kindergarten issue. Technically, there is no homework. You can't fool me, though. I know there are plenty of kindergarten parents out there who are secretly teaching their kids after hours to colour, paste and use scissors in order to get ahead of my kids so that, when jobs are being handed out in the year 2018, their precious darlings will be the doctors and lawyers of the world while mine, still grappling with mucilage and long division, will be waiting for latecomers to get their asses out of Safeway so they can start washing the floors.

Can't give up. Must find green snack. I bet there's a convenience store somewhere in town that has a jar of beef jerky that's long past its best-before date. Naw. Can't turn my kids against convenience stores. They'll be working half their lives in them.

I briefly consider buying two $2 bags of jelly beans and separating the green ones. I would have, too, but the kids would have ended up with about four each. Cough drops? Too medicinal. Pickles? Too much like vegetables. Who would have thought kindergarten would be so hard? With the store about to close, I start looking for stuff with green packaging. Pringles sour cream and onion chips come in a gorgeous green can. The kids love chips. And, if I looked hard enough I'd probably find some sort of potato-related vitamin in them. Sold! On a roll now, I finally notice a tiny box of green Jell-O powder. Yes! We'll have to make it from scratch, mind you, but it can't be that hard. To complete the triple play, I spy a box of Wrigley's Doublemint gum. Green as hell. Sold! I get to the checkout about a minute before they start turning off the tills. I'm not exactly gloating about the brilliance of my choices, but I did my best, and I'm prepared to live with the consequences.

I pay. I collect my change. I start walking out of the now-closed store. About 10 steps from the door, I see a woman out of the corner of my eye. She's eating an apple. A GREEN apple. A delicious, nutritious, vitamin-laden snack that's high in fibre, contains no artificial flavours or preservatives and comes in an eco-friendly package.

Doh!

October 6, 2001

Some dads just can't Handel music class

In the greatest musical triumph since his guest appearance as solo trianglist with the local community band, area resident Mac Relluf successfully filled in at his kids' music class Wednesday evening.

"I survived. I don't know how, but I survived," Relluf said, clearly shaken, moments after the hour-long ordeal.

Relluf's presence was required when his wife had to work on the night of their boys' weekly piano lesson. The music program they're enrolled in demands "hands-on" parental involvement, so simply dropping the children off at the music teacher's door (and perhaps nipping downtown for a quick pint) was out of the question.

"Not that I'd actually do that," Relluf claimed.

During the week, Relluf's wife diligently practises songs, rhythm patterns and piano scales with the children. Relluf uses this time to wash the dishes. As a result, his musical education is somewhat limited.

"I don't know C sharp from sharp cheddar," the local man volunteered.

Another quality in which Relluf is lacking is patience, sources said. Two years ago, when the twins were five, Relluf was left with the difficult – some might say impossible – task of overseeing a practice session when the children were "not in the mood."

"I'm still scarred from the experience," Relluf contended.

Also scarred is one wooden stick, used to point at the notes as the children played. It's now taped together, but bears signs that it was broken in two over a man's knee during a *pianissimo* swearing session in the basement following 20 minutes of inattentive behaviour by the young Liszt twins upstairs.

Complicating matters is the unique method of musical education the family has subscribed to. Rather than simply giving the music notes their proper names – C, G, F and so on – the notes are associated with characters. F, for instance, is "a fireman whose name is Fred," C is a "creepy, crawly critter," and so on.

Having to memorize these names is simply beyond the abilities of Mr. Relluf, who is more apt to stammer "E is an . . . earthy, earnest elephant" than the correct "elegant elk named Edith." Left in charge one evening, Relluf simply forgot "G is a grouchy, grumpy groundhog" and blurted out "G is a ghastly . . . greenish gnome."

"I thought I was thinking quickly on my feet," Relluf argued. The children's howls of disapproval suggested otherwise, neighbours confirmed.

Studies have shown that teaching music to young children can be more stressful than moving, public speaking and taking a polygraph test, according to the Musical Educators' Society of Saskatchewan (MESS).

"It's not as simple as playing the triangle," warned MESS director Scarlatti Nachtmusic.

"You're telling me?" Relluf said when told of the research.

Tension grew as Wednesday night's lesson loomed. The children started losing confidence in their father's ability when he had to ask them for directions to the teacher's house. When they got there, the class had already started, heightening the disorientation.

"When we walk in the door the first thing one of my kids says is 'What number are we?'" Relluf said later. "I had no idea what he was talking about. But he keeps repeating 'What number are we? What number are we?' until he's practically screaming."

All Relluf could do was shush his child and smile weakly at all the mothers in the otherwise quiet room, convinced they were cataloguing his deficiencies as a father, husband and music educator. It turned out that the mats the kids kneel on are numbered. "Luckily, there were only two left, so it wasn't hard to figure out which ones were ours," said Relluf.

The lesson began. The teacher clapped a pattern. The kids whipped out a collection of bread tags, pipe cleaners and drinking straws to diagram the rhythm. "I haven't been so confused since Grade 11 trigonometry," said Relluf.

Then they played the song they had spent the week learning. Most of the moms pointed to the notes as the kids played. Relluf said he would have done this, too, if he "could've remembered which one was Fred and which one was the stupid anteater – or is it an aardvark?"

Instead, he just stood there trying to look like he was thinking of something musically important, like Chopin's mother-in-law's maiden name. Later, the teacher went over the following week's assignment, warning the class that a certain note, which they used to play with a certain finger, would now be played with a different finger.

"By then, the only fingers I was thinking about were the ones I use to twist the caps off beer bottles," Relluf offered.

Despite the trauma, Relluf said he was trying to look on the bright side. "Thank God I don't have daughters in ballet."

October 25, 2003

It's not a sick joke; it's the flu

It takes a village to raise a child, they say. I'd like to know where the village was on Monday at approximately 3 a.m. when we were awakened with the following words from one of our kids:

"I don't feel very . . . woooooof."

Thus was the flu season officially under way. Nothing is more disorienting at three in the morning than sudden child vomiting. You could go through basic training with the Green Berets and still not be prepared for it. One minute, you're dreaming of, well, never mind. The next, you're dealing with strange, random, urgent thoughts flying out of the darkness. Where's the paper towel . . . ? Should I start cleaning this up now or run for the puke bucket . . . ? Maybe if I don't open my eyes, my wife won't notice I'm here. . . . How much work am I going to miss because of this, and is that a good thing or a bad thing . . . ?

Your first impulse, though, is to stand there and shake your fist at the heavens.

"Why me?" you'd yell at the firmament. "Why didst thou smote me with a fluey grade schooler? Don't thou knowest I have a 10 a.m. appointment I simply cannot misseth?"

(And, of course, you also feel awful that your sweet little child is sick, blah, blah, blah, yada, yada, yada.)

After the initial triage and cleanup, it's back to Slumberland for a refreshing hour or so of shut-eye. By the glum light of dawn, however, the wreckage of the week-to-come already lies before you.

Chances are, both parents work (if only to sustain a lavish lifestyle of four pizza nights a year and a trip to Disneyland once every lifetime or so). In that case, you find yourself having NASA-calibre planning meetings with your spouse while rushing around the kitchen serving breakfast to the kid who isn't sick, making his lunch and loading his backpack. You have conversations like, "I'll go in first and work until 10:18, then I'll come home so you can make it in by 11:09, but don't forget I have that two o'clock thing, so if you could be back home by 1:43, say, that should give me enough time to . . . enough time to . . ."

Enough time to bend over and kiss your week goodbye. The reality of the situation is that things were too complicated even before the flu struck. If the week isn't organized down to the spare minute, chaos ensues. One stumble and you're off the moving sidewalk of life and lying on the floor in the airport terminal of hell.

Keeping up with homework, for example, has become our second job. I don't know how this happened. I thought I graduated from Grade 2 in 1971. Apparently not, since it's now my avocation to find out what that sheet of incomplete phonics questions is doing in the bottom of the culprit's knapsack, to interrogate the suspect in order to determine if this is, indeed, homework and, if so, which questions need to be finished and by when. Usually, the accused is as vague in his answers as a career criminal.

Parent: Don't you have a spelling test on Friday?

Child: Damien fell off the swings today!

Okay, kid. Maybe you can make a complete sentence from the following words: hit, bat, Dad, head, on, with, the, a.

Thanks to homework, I won't be seeing a primetime TV show for the next 10 years. I know I'm not missing much, but the gang from *Friends* is going to look awfully funny by 2013.

Thanks to homework, making supper has now become slightly more difficult than juggling chainsaws. Where's the village when you're pulling your hair out trying to explain to a young scholar the mystical connection between $12 - 7 = 5$ and $7 + 5 = 12$ (without actually blurting out the stupid answers, which is what you'd really like to do), while the pot of Sidekicks noodles you put on the stove is boiling over?

I'm telling you, it's too hard. If this were a virtual reality simulator instead of real life, the guys in the lab coats would be shutting the system down and pulling you out before it's too late.

And this is life on a good week. On a bad week, when fluish Thing One has spent the day on the couch watching TV, life really gets interesting. That's when Thing Two comes home with the first load of the schoolwork his brother has missed. Your mission, after the stove is cleaned up, is to have him complete six hours of reading, colouring, clipping and pasting in the remaining half hour of the day. You'd feel sorry for the poor child, but in a delicious bit of irony, you're facing the exact same situation at work tomorrow.

Have we raised the bar high enough here? By these standards, the ideal parent is an octopus with an education degree and the stamina of a triathlete.

Oh, but even the bad days come to an end. It's 9 p.m. now, 18 hours after the you-know-what hit the floor. You're doing what you're always doing at this time of the day – enjoying a cup of chamomile tea and reading a good book. Hah! Just kidding! You're washing dishes, of course. (When I finally crack up – and I will, believe me – it will be at the sink while scrubbing a frying pan.)

At the same time, you're feeling guilty that the kids rarely get five servings of fruit or vegetables per day, and that somehow, under your watch, they usually miss the recommended daily allotment of 30 minutes of vigorous exercise. You vow tomorrow will be different. Tomorrow you'll be more patient and less selfish. Tomorrow you'll find a way to make brussels sprouts palatable, math fun and bologna nutritious. Tomorrow you'll . . . what's that noise? Why, if it isn't Thing Two throwing up.

November 8, 2003

Learning curve ahead: proceed with caution

As a sensitive New Age parent of two children in Grade 3, I appreciate the value of homework. I just wish they'd finish it before they got home.

Long before I became a sensitive New Age parent (or SNAP), I successfully completed the requirements of Grade 3. I can prove it. I have my Grade 3 report card right here. The last paragraph, signed by the Principal Himself, reads as follows: "This is to certify that Cam Fuller has completed Unit 12 of the work in Division I and will begin working at Unit 1 in Division II next September." It was a good report card, if not a stellar one. I had zero absences. None. Also, I'm pleased to report, I received an A in "word attack skills." I've been fighting words ever since.

"Cam is a good student," my teacher wrote. "He works very well in class. He does like to talk though at times."

Talk? Talk about bad luck. Little did I know that Grade 3 was not quite behind me – that, some 32 years later, I would be back in Grade 3, in spirit if not in body. There's more work to be done, it seems.

Oh, the books are different, but the subjects are the same: reading, writing, arithmetic, spelling. I'm not the one doing the work, of course, but parents these days are expected to be much more involved in the process. Perhaps my memory is selective, but I can't recall my parents ever helping me with my homework – unless you count my mom taking a break from peeling potatoes to sharpen my pencil with her paring knife.

Replay a scene from a typical school night last winter. I'm in the basement with one child, writing $9 + 3 =$ _ and $6 + 3 =$ _ and $9 - 6 =$ _ on a chalkboard while my wife is upstairs listening to the other child read his book. In 20 minutes, we'll switch. After that, we'll convene to go over tomorrow's spelling bee words.

We're very proud of our 1:1 student-teacher ratio here at C'mon Learning Centre. And not a single education degree in the faculty! We're lucky the kids don't sue us for malpractice. As far as teaching technique goes, don't look to me for inspiration. What I lack in patience I make up for in incompetence. Confronted by a list of synonyms, a recent attempt at reverse psychology was rather brief:

Me: I could do these in my sleep.

My kid: Then why don't you fall asleep and do them?

I suppose I could look at the experience as quality time spent with our children. But, if I may be allowed to whisper the truth, I don't enjoy it. Explaining to a frustrated child why "there" is not the same as "their" or "they're" when he would much rather be watching *SpongeBob SquarePants* is like rolling a rock up a hill. (Especially when you wouldn't mind watching *SpongeBob SquarePants* yourself.)

But no, there's work to do. One evening in Grade 1, I found myself building an eight-sided object out of construction paper so my kid could count how many edges, corners and planes it contained. It took about half an hour of painstaking drawing, cutting and taping. By the time I was done I had broken new ground in geometry.

The work itself is the least of my worries these days, however. It's finding out what the assignment is and when it's due back that's the challenge.

Getting these young scholars to divulge the truth is like interrogating captured prisoners in wartime. All you get is name, rank and serial number. Why would they volunteer information that will have a direct and negative impact on their precious liberty?

Getting books back to school is another problem. I swear they disappear. Set them down, walk away, turn around and they're simply gone. Then morning comes and it's time to fill the backpacks. The following is an actual conversation that took place this week while I was rushing to get the kids to school on time:

Me: Where's your schoolbook – the one you were working on last night?

Kid: Blank stare.

Me: Where's your schoolbook – the one you were working on last night?

Kid: Dad, you have shaving cream on your chin.

Me: Where's your schoolbook?

Kid: Which one?

"Learning can be fun when it's a family thing," a bright and cheery TV commercial proclaimed recently. In a perfect world, perhaps so. In my world, I find more comfort in the Parent's Serenity Prayer:

"God grant me the serenity to supervise homework while trying to turn a frozen chicken brick into an edible supper in the next 35 minutes, the courage not to blurt out all the answers and the wisdom to know that no matter what happens, it's All My Fault."

I'm starting to see the attraction of those private tutorial franchises. One ad features a mom looking annoyed when she hears noises upstairs at bedtime. She barges in on her kids and finds the older child reading to the younger one. Reading! A miracle! Just last week he was using books to set public buildings on fire but now he's reading them! Cue the violin music. Close-up on mom's face, her eyes welling with tears of joy and pride. Thank you, Klass Klowns Tutorial Services International! Thank you so much! Now, can you tell me how many edges there are in a hexiplane?

October 2, 2004

Fate delivers a tart lesson or two

The saskatoon berry tarts were for me. Yes, I had purchased enough for the kids to try – but only one each and only to prevent the inevitable caterwauling that would have ensued if I'd avoided sharing and gotten caught.

Naturally, I hid the rest. That's right. I hide food.

The idea never even occurred to me before I had kids. Even after the first couple of years of blessed parenting, the children were far too young to notice the double standard that played out in the kitchen every mealtime: Steak for me. And for you? Visualize whirled peas. Mmm. You love them! Yes, you do! Yes, you do!

But when those little hungry eyes start gazing at your teriyaki chicken wings from behind a bowl of Gerber's Vegetable Medley, you know the gravy train has reached the end of the line. It's time to hide the good stuff.

Is it my fault you forgot there was one more brownie? While your back was turned, I poured myself a glass of milk, palmed the brownie, hid it on a plate in the cupboard and nibbled it down with brilliantly subtle bites as I pretended to tidy up the kitchen. Why, it was almost as if that delicious fudgy square had never existed at all. Abracadabra. Behold the Houdini of hidden food.

I can't recall when I started hiding food, but I suspect it has something to do with potato chips. Something to do with reaching up to the high shelf for the bag of Old Dutch that you know is there, only to find that it isn't. Only to find that Exhibit A has already been consumed by Kid B, as evinced by the empty chip bag in Garbage Can C. It doesn't help when Kid B has such a keen interest in potato chips that he can be sitting at home and still hear the crinkle of the bag as it's tossed into the shopping cart.

One minute you're gingerly feeding premature newborn twins, the next you're hiding snacks from them. It's touching, this Circle of Life.

I'll never forget the illicit thrill of drinking Coke out of a coffee mug for the first time. I did this to prevent the inevitable question: "Why can't I have some?" The only answer to this question, of course, is: "Because you can't." Children are rarely satisfied with this answer, or its equivalent: "Because I said so." They counter with the big guns: "Please?" Followed by a volley of "Please, please, please, please, please?" If you break down, you've set the precedent. From then on, it's Coke for everyone, anytime they feel like it. This is anarchy. But sipping your Coke from a coffee cup brings harmony to a troubled world.

I can't pretend I didn't feel guilty the first time I relocated the chip bag to the downstairs desk drawer. Or the first time I ordered Chinese food late at night and kept the leftovers in the downstairs fridge where the kids never look. But I also can't pretend that it didn't feel wonderfully satisfying to regain control.

Is it right to deny your children the very snacks you eat yourself? Of course it is! What possible advantage could there be in being an adult (other than, you know, getting to drive a car) if it doesn't entitle you to unfettered access to the treats you've purchased with your own hard-earned money? Besides, the kids don't need all that sugar and salt. Neither do you, of course, but at least you know the meaning of the word moderation. Left to their own devices, a well-balanced meal planned by kids would consist of beef jerky (the protein component), popcorn (the starch), Doritos (the vegetable) and aerosol whipped cream sprayed directly into the mouth (dessert). These are not rational beings we're dealing with.

Not rational, but definitely smart. My hiding techniques had become so routine that I finally slipped up. I made the same mistake of every habitual criminal; I got complacent. Rather than take the trouble to return a partial bag of chips to the desk drawer, I thought I was being clever by dropping them behind the stereo speaker. That way, I could simply reach over when no one was looking. But no. A few days later, Kid B caught a glimpse and bounded over to investigate. "Hah! You're mine," he said to the chips, thrusting his hand into the bag. Lucky for me, he was too excited to ask why the chips were even there. I wonder how many times he came back to see if more had sprouted.

I was almost caught because I'd forgotten the basic difference between adults and kids. Adults are taller. That's what makes the fancy-dishes cupboard above the stove so valuable. This is where we keep such essentials as the wine charms and the decorative butter spreaders with the fancy handles that look like reindeer or jackalope. Believe me, a world without wine charms is not one I want to live in. The fancy-dishes cupboard happened to be the best place to hide those last two saskatoon berry tarts. They were things of beauty purchased as an extra special treat from a real bakery, the pastry golden brown, the filling sweet but not too sweet.

I can't remember why I opened the fancy-dishes cupboard that day, only the shocking sight that presented itself. I could almost hear the scary violin music from *Psycho* as I opened the door to discover my saskatoon berry tarts wearing brilliant ermine coats of mold. I put them there weeks before. Then forgot about them; I hadn't hidden them from the kids but from myself.

Okay, so maybe I deserved it. Maybe someone was teaching me a lesson about not sharing. But did two innocent, delicious tarts have to be sacrificed? That's just mean.

April 29, 2006

What to expect when you're not expected home

The cookie supply was depleted and only a surge of new chocolatey wafers would bring our calorie count back up to pre-invasion levels. I called in the Dad's Chocolatey Coated Variety Pack, but not without some misgivings. The poor thing was about to be left unprotected in hostile territory.

It's the kids. They're old enough now to come right home without marinating in the after-school program for 90 minutes each day. They get to be alone without supervision. Fun for them; not so much fun for the Goodie Rings.

In a perfect world, the latchkeys would start doing homework the minute they got in the door, stopping only to have a healthy snack of spinach juice and whole-wheat crackers. I realized that wasn't going to happen when I came home a bit early this week to find one of them frying a pound of hamburger. On the bright side, he wasn't trying to see if the blender would grind up Bic pens. He wasn't playing "let's put all the cutlery in the microwave" or trying to find out if you really can float down from the roof by hanging on to an umbrella.

But the prospect of tweenagers home alone does raise a couple of concerns. You want them to be safe. That's the first thing. Definitely. Nothing is more important, not even those delicious oatmeal coconut cookies. I can't decide if I like them more with a tall glass of cold milk or dipped into a hot cup of coffee, just long enough to soften that coating of sweet, dark. . . . Where was I? Oh yes, my innocent, helpless babies.

I suspect the house will have to be childproofed again. The last time we went through this they were toddlers and our house ended up looking like a war zone. The high chairs, lest they be climbed, were hung from big hooks on the wall when we weren't using them. There were homemade sticks screwed into the edges of the countertop to keep the drawers from being opened and pillaged. We spent an alarming amount of money on a cheap, plastic baby gate. It was soon torn off its hinges and replaced by a tasteful slab of plywood. It's long gone now, but the holes from the screws that held its hinges to the oak newel post remain. I look at them every time I go downstairs. And they look back.

Now, with digital cable and the internet just itching to dump a mind-blowing array of questionable material on our doorstep, I wish things were still baby-gate simple. Tween-proofing the television became a top priority when the kids recently discovered the television show *CSI* (unofficial slogan: "Sexy, Naked and Dead? Cool!") and the TV channel Spike (unofficial slogan: "Offensive in So Many Ways"). Luckily, it's simple to block the bad shows and channels. Unfortunately, I can't watch the Food Network now without entering my pin number. (Just between you and me, it's ****.)

As for the computer, I've become a human Net Nanny. When I need to know what they're up to, I can materialize behind them like a ninja in a kung fu movie. The trick is to see what they're looking at without them knowing, because if they knew you didn't trust them (which you don't), they might get offended and, just to spite you, start looking at stuff they wouldn't have looked at otherwise. Naturally, this would be All Your Fault. Peace in the Middle East is easier to maintain.

But you can't always be at home. That's when you need some of that child-safe internet software. I prefer Net Caveman 2.0: a length of two-by-four to smash the computer to bits.

Luckily, we're not going into this alone. The Canada Safety Council has plenty of advice for leaving your kids on their own. The Canada Safety Council should be consulted whenever you're going into a potentially peril-ous situation, like swimming after eating or fighting with your spouse. ("Of course I wasn't thinking of going fishing this weekend, honey!") The council's fact sheet on leaving kids home alone is an invaluable resource for worried parents. At least, it would be in a world where kids don't let the toilet overflow without telling anyone.

Here's how some of the safety council's advice looks on paper compared to real life.

Official Advice: "Set firm rules, with clear dos and don'ts." (Like, "Don't eat all the cookies," perhaps.)

Real Life: "But they were so yummy!"

Official Advice: "Specify how his or her time is to be spent." (Like, "No TV.")

Real Life: "But 'Xtreme Skateboard Concussions' is on at 4:30!"

Official Advice: "Test smoke alarms to make sure they all work."

Real Life: No problem there. I know ours works from when I burned the toast. That's why I took the battery out.

None of this solves the cookie problem, either. That's why I've invented the Cookie Safe. It's a cookie jar that can only be opened when the user answers a math or spelling or geography question tailored to the child's age. The only problem is that they might get frustrated and take the Caveman 2.0 stick to it. And even if it works, they might steal all the cookies, like dishonest people with newspaper boxes. Come to think of it, you might as well leave the cookies in the cupboard. Fig Newtons, though. The Dad's Variety Pack will have to be hidden.

This too shall pass, I know. The kids will do great on their own. They'll be safe (once they stop leaving the key in the lock). They'll develop self-confidence and learn to do things on their own (as long as it doesn't involve turning off the lights when they leave a room, let's be reasonable here).

The sad thing is that they're going to grow up, and I'm going to grow old. Eventually, they'll be worried about *me* being home alone. If they hide my cookies, I'll freak.

September 15, 2007

Man shows signs of 'Almost-Empty-Nest Syndrome'

A local father was shocked to learn recently that his services are no longer required.

After 16 years of parenting, the middle-aged man woke up one day, ate breakfast and went to work. He was stunned at how little was required of him that morning. And the morning after that. And the morning after that.

"My kids didn't need lunches. They didn't need help finding their books. They didn't need their backpacks packed. There were no shoes to tie. And they drove themselves to school," he said in an interview.

It's a day he thought he would never see in his lifetime. When his sons came home from the hospital, they were tiny and vulnerable. They weighed less than the alternator from a Kia. They were shorter than a torque wrench. They were utterly helpless.

They couldn't tell time, which explains why they woke up every two hours to see if it was morning yet. They couldn't dress themselves. They didn't know the rule about wearing white pants after Labour Day. They had no idea what was trending on Twitter. It was pathetic, really.

As for eating, forget it. Their mouths were so small they had to be finger-fed, a process in which milk from a syringe is pumped down a tube taped to the parent's pinky. They couldn't walk to the fridge, much less open the door and stuff themselves with cold cuts.

They didn't even know English – the most popular language on earth. And yet both their parents were fluent. *Yes, they were! Yes, they were, you little-widdle, oodlie-woodlie woos!*

Left with two new humans to prevent from dying, the parents had no choice but to put their own needs and interests on hold. Whatever they used to do in their free time was abandoned in favour of midnight diaper runs, 4 a.m. feedings and cruel and unusual torture at the hands of purple dinosaurs and sadistic aliens called Teletubbies.

For the father, the lifestyle change was shocking and abrupt. Before kids, his garage was an adult-sized tree house. After kids, it was a place to park cars. Before kids, he always used to have some sort of project going on. If the deck needed rebuilding on a sunny summer Saturday, he'd just rebuild the damn deck. But with infants, and then toddlers, and then preschoolers, and then schoolers underfoot, projects were undoable.

In time, the man forgot what it was like to read an entire magazine article without being interrupted 10 times. He forgot what it was like to eat sitting down. He forgot what it was like to wake up due to natural causes.

"It takes a few years, but you get used to it," the man insisted. "There's nothing like Aqua-Tots on Saturday mornings and doing the hokey-pokey in the pool with carpet-chested Sasquatch fathers."

But time went by, just like Stephen Hawking said it would, and before long the man's children could swim on their own. That ended swimming. And once they could ride bikes, bike riding wasn't very interesting. And as soon as they got old enough to go to the same movies as their parents, they didn't want to go to the same movies as their parents.

The clincher was driver education. It was inconceivable to the local father that the same human beings who used to soak their Hot Wheels in vinegar and baking soda would now be operating 1:1 scale motor vehicles on public roads. But he did his duty and taught his former infants how to drive, he said.

And that was it. They got their licences, and he's barely seen them since.

"Apparently, they now know everything they need to know. My work here is done," the man said. He was sprawled on the couch downstairs, killing the last few hours before bedtime.

It's not unusual for parents to feel "out of sorts," when their children are old enough to fend for themselves, experts say. "A loss of the nurturing identity is the hallmark of Almost-Empty-Nest Syndrome," says a pamphlet that could well be from the Mayo Clinic or some other important-sounding institution. Sufferers need to rebuild their personalities and rediscover who they were before they had children, according to adult development researchers.

"I tried that," said the man. "I used to have hobbies. I used to take photos and develop them myself." Now, of course, digitization has rendered the home darkroom obsolete.

"I used to make my own beer, too," the man added. Unfortunately, ingredients have become hard to find. The man recently went to a wine kit store and asked for dried light malt extract.

"Yeah, no. Haven't seen that since the home-brewing fad of the early 1990s," the owner said.

His evenings now free and empty, the man is considering exciting new hobbies, like string art and wood burning. In the meantime, he plans to continue wandering around his empty house. "*X-Files* on tonight?" he said.

October 21, 2012

Chapter 6

In Over My Head

Some guys are just handy. They know how to do everything. I should envy them but I don't. Some guys don't know how to do anything and don't care. Them, I envy. For it is caring that leads one into doom.

I come from the phylum *Fixatious problematica*. I know just enough to get in over my head. My handiness started in childhood with bicycles. I could fix a flat and change a tire all by myself. It never occurred to me to ask my dad to do it. I was the last of six kids. He really wasn't looking for father-son bonding projects by then.

But he did pass on his thrifty gene to me. I hate the idea of paying one of those handy guys to do a repair or renovation that I might be able to do myself. And that's how *Fixatious problematica* found himself at the Mediclinic one Saturday evening rather than at home making supper.

Up to that point, it had been a splendid day. Installing vinyl floor tiles in the furnace room is a perfect project for a do-it-yourselfer. If you do it right, it looks great. If you don't, who's going to notice?

After about eight hours on my knees worshipping the god of thrift, I was almost finished. The tiles were straight. The floor was smooth. And I was pretty much spent. I had one tile left, a tricky one because it needed a hole in it for the floor drain. Like a gang member in *West Side Story*, I whipped out my razor knife. *Gonna cut you, tile. Gonna cut you good.*

And I did. My cut-out for the drain was dramatic and convincing – until the knife slipped, and I sliced through my thumb. I believe the instructions advised against that. (Mediclinic tip: bleeding on the counter can reduce your wait time by up to 10 per cent.) Okay, so I might have lost a thumb tendon and the ability to hitchhike with my left hand. But I gained valuable experience both in flooring and knife safety.

"Cut toward your buddy, not your body. You can always get another buddy." Sage advice provided by a handy brother-in-law. Provided a few days too late, but still.

What motivates the do-it-yourself guy?

- The desire for knowledge. He has always wanted to learn about grout, so he actually embraces that tiling project.

- The desire to save money. Paying a guy like you to do something that a guy like you can (probably) do yourself seems uneconomical.

Not that it always goes smoothly. So, as in most of life's endeavours, it's great to have an outlet for the pent-up frustration of a home improvement project gone wrong. For me, that means writing about my forehead-slapping misadventures. A simple column won't cure a soft tissue injury, but it can be soothing in its own way.

That's when I put aside the cordless drill (can't find the right drill bit anyway) and start processing words. For me, a freshly painted wall is just as satisfying as a computer screen covered in paragraphs. And there's no bloodshed. Usually.

It can't hurt to be more careful at home

Can I learn something from my latest self-inflicted injury? OUCH. When I went to type "self-inflicted" just now, I had to look down at my keyboard to find the hyphen key. I had to do this in slow motion because my neck is sore and looking down hurts.

So there's a lesson right there: You should learn to touch-type so you can find the hyphen without looking for it when you do something really stupid and hurt your neck.

Oh, I'm just full of new insights this week. I now realize how heavy my head is, how much work the thin string of my neck has to do to keep that cement-filled beach ball from lolling from one side to another. I never knew, for example, how many muscles are involved in simply rolling over in bed. Now that it hurts so much that it cuts off my breathing and causes my eyes to water, I can look back fondly on all the carefree rolling I used to do.

Truly, I have a greater appreciation for the mechanical wonder that a properly functioning human body really is. Try shoulder-checking (God, another hyphen). You really have to stretch to do that. My version of shoulder-checking has been reduced to thinking, "Nobody had better be there because I don't care anymore."

And all this because I chose to lift a patio table onto my back rather than asking for help. I was going to put it under the deck for the winter. I did the lifting part OK, but then the back end of the table hit the railing while I was going down the stairs and levered my head forward suddenly. It was mere discomfort at first. The searing pain came later.

Do women do stupid things like this? I don't think so. They might slip on ice or turn an ankle on a curb, but those are accidents. What I did was more of a "mancident" – an easily avoided injury caused by bullheadedness and overconfidence.

I shared my story with a fellow man this week, knowing that another male would identify with the had-to-do-it-myself (four hyphens, I'm dying right now) ethos. He waited until my gums stopped flapping and then launched into a better story of his own about standing on a swivel stool above a staircase. It did not go well.

Most mancidents are hardly worth mentioning, like the blood blister I got last week when the skin on my thumb got pinched between two pieces of wood I was screwing together. You gasp, you swear and then you have to compose yourself enough to reverse the drill and unscrew the screw to get your skin out of there. But it hurts for, what, an hour? No big deal.

It's the maybe-more-serious (more hyphens) injuries that are of greater concern, the ones that make you think, "Maybe I'm really hurt here." You try to put it out of your mind, but you can't. All you can think is "Should I be seeking medical attention?" The debate begins.

It would be stupid not to get this checked out. But I hate to overreact. But it hurts more than most of the bad things I do to myself. But do I want to spend three hours in the Mediclinic to find out it's nothing? Maybe it'll clear up in a few days. I'll just tough it out.

But isn't that what Gary tried to do? And look at him now, all shrivelled up like last year's carrot, unable to work, depressed, alone, broke. If only he'd gone to the doctor after hitting his thumb with that hammer. Maybe my neck thing is the start of a lifelong injury. "Yup, had this shooting pain down my left arm for 30-odd years after trying to lift a table. Just learned to live with it."

I feel the urge to pray. "God, if you heal me, I'll start promoting safety."

That's it! Mancident-Prevention Week. Damn, another hyphen.

October 14, 2017

House takes Saskatchewan man hostage

Authorities in this quiet north-central community are baffled by what they call the first case of house-human abduction in North America.

Local homeowner Sam Router was last seen in early February hauling 32 boxes of new tongue-and-groove flooring into the basement of his modest bi-level. It was a cold Saturday afternoon. He hasn't been seen since.

"The drilling, sawing and cussing indicate a human presence. We have reason to believe he's still in the house," said Makita Township Police Chief Patrick DeWalt.

Router, 47, has lived in the 30-year-old house for the past 19 years. Since that time, he has stripped wallpaper, removed carpeting, changed light fixtures, painted doors, replaced trim, painted the kitchen, rebuilt the sun deck, painted the living room, fixed the fencing, painted the bedrooms, insulated and drywalled the garage, painted the living room again, installed flooring, grouted tile, painted the kitchen again, replaced the front gate, painted the living room again, painted the siding, painted the bedrooms again, replaced interior doors, painted the doors again, scraped and stained the deck, scraped and stained the deck again and scraped and stained the deck yet again.

People familiar with the case say Router lived a fairly normal life despite the constant construction, even finding time to keep a day job, maintain a marriage and start a family. It's not known if he had any other interests.

Despite the amount of work accomplished, Router had barely touched the house's lower level, friends say. As the years went by, the downstairs carpeting became worn and tattered, particularly after Router insisted on never getting a pet, which led to the family getting a dog. And then another dog.

After overseeing a major kitchen renovation, Router told friends he was "sick and tired" of all the labour, upheaval and expense. He stated that it would be "years" before he undertook another project. It's believed, however, that his spouse had other plans.

Sources say that Mrs. Router was "sick and tired" of the carpet downstairs and that it "had to go." She wouldn't return calls seeking comment. But the Times Dispatch has learned that what began as a straightforward flooring conversion took a path into the bizarre. Router confided in friends that the house was becoming more and more demanding and that he had "a bad feeling" heading into yet another home improvement project.

Even so, in late January, he donned his Work Wearhouse canvas pants, took a razor knife from the garage and headed downstairs to deal with the carpet. Builders say it's likely that Router would have immediately encountered "Smoothedge" – long strips of plywood embedded with small nails as sharp as a kitten's claws. In a basement, Smoothedge would have been glued and nailed into the concrete pad under the carpet, making removal a time-consuming and labour-intensive endeavour. That would have been followed by cutting the dirty, smelly carpet into strips for removal, along with the dusty foam underlay.

"For the kind of amateur you're describing, we're talking 10 to 15 man-hours of hard work," said area contractor Mel (Big) Kenny. "It's what we call a weekend-killer."

A string of similar weekends would have faced the man, consuming all his free time and confining him to the house, much like a character in a Stephen King novel – a shut-in forever doomed to search for his misplaced tape measure.

After installing the new flooring, experts say, Router would have experienced the eerie "while-we're" phenomenon. "While-we're" stretches manageable projects into big, endless ones: "While we're doing the floor, we might as well paint. While we're painting, we might as well get new doors. While we're getting new doors, we might as well get new door casings. While we're getting new door casings, we might as well change the baseboards. While we're changing the baseboards, we might as well replace the light fixtures."

And on and on.

Acting on a tip that the supernatural might be involved, the Times Dispatch contacted local psychic Bosch Padsander, who analyzed a Google Street View photograph of the Router home. "It's not that he won't stop working, it's that he can't. The house won't let him," Padsander confirmed.

Police have set up a perimeter around the scene of the hostage-taking. But they are wary of entering the home lest they also be put to work filling endless nail holes and sanding doors.

However, they did collect a piece of evidence from the large pile of renovation rubbish in the front yard. Scratched into a broken piece of baseboard is a chilling warning: "Redo my bathrooms or the guy gets it."

The investigation continues.

April 16, 2011

In the company of men

A roof-raising was called for. Two days in the trees, up to your rafters in rafters, building a roof where there wasn't one before, on top of a cabin that wasn't there before.

I don't know anything about roofs. But I agreed to help my buddy because that's what buddies do. And it never hurts to have a great big favour in the bank.

The Pile: On the driveway sat a tall stack of roof trusses, a geometric marvel of two-by-fours and two-by-sixes forming triangles-within-triangles, nature's strongest shape. There were 21 of them. They had to be evenly spaced over 40 feet. If they weren't square to the walls, the roof would end up looking like a sideways cap on the head of a rapper. Math was involved. Good old-fashioned measurements ending with things like "three-eighths" and "11-sixteenths." I've spent a lot of time squinting at tape measures, trying to find these amazing fractions. They never seem to present themselves. Thank goodness for . . .

The Men: There were worker bees in this hive of activity, and there were a couple of guys who were actual builders; men who use their hands to make things that last a long time. They have tools. They know fractions.

It's an impressive thing to be in the company of men. Their boots thunder on the floor when they walk, hammers dangling from the holster of their tool belts: gunfighters on a chipboard frontier. They crack excellent jokes, scattering sarcasm like shotgun pellets. They swear like it's a second language and give real-time updates on what's happening to the chili they had for lunch. They're crude yet precise, measuring and marking important lines with flat-sided pencils and punctuating their decisions with rapid shots from the air nailer.

The Task: We had to get the rafters onto the roof and hand them off to the men. Without the use of helicopters, the labourer has no choice but to use ladders. Trusses are heavy, but the real problem is that they bend easily. Imagine picking a fish off the ground that's almost too heavy to lift and then have it start squirming. Now carry it 20 or 30 feet, then up six or eight stairs onto the deck, then turn it upside down, then push it up as you climb an extension ladder. It's the kind of thing that you get tired of after doing it once. The thought of 20 more just shuts your brain down. Not-thinking becomes a survival tactic. Keep the machine working. Eighteen. Fifteen. The sweat pours, the muscles protest. Ten. Five. Mommy.

The Tools: Did I mention the air nailer? It's the scariest thing there is. It shoots real nails as fast as you can pull the trigger. It's impossible to look at an air nailer without having one of those "wouldn't it be awful if" daydreams about blasting a nail right through your own kneecap. The adrenaline rush from that thought is better than any cup of Thermos coffee.

The pace of the work is a bell curve. There's lots of standing around to start with as things get figured out. You hear lots of conversations that go like, "It's only a sixteenth out."

"Yeah, but a sixteenth over 40 feet . . ."

You visualize trains derailing, cars going over cliffs, Wright Brothers airplanes crashing – total chaos, in other words, all because of that first bad sixteenth.

Then the work starts, instantly at full speed. The men need material. If you don't keep the wheels turning, you'll get run over by them. Lunch won't occur until three. Supper, not till dark. In the flurry, you resist the urge to look up and check the progress, afraid to be disappointed. But when you do take a peek, you see row after row of arrow-straight lumber. We did that? Amazing.

The Next Day: Time to put skin on the skeleton. Up the ladder with countless sheets of galvanized metal. You're afraid the sharp edges will cut your gloves. Then you look over at the man beside you, and he's hoisting his end with bare hands. Hey, I work in an office, okay? Another dozen hours of climbing, lifting and drilling. Seamlessly, every worker finds a job that keeps the system running smoothly. Bodies are pushed harder than they should be, but not quite enough to break. Rain's coming. Gotta get 'er done.

The Fatigue: It's complete, universal, sumptuous in its own way and bizarrely satisfying. A "good tired," as they say. It was hard but not bad. Best of all was the odd sense of *déja vu* that went with the work. Because, really, how different was all this from when you were a kid building treehouses and playing guns with your friends? Hanging in the air is hanging in the air whether you're 10 and three-eighths or 40 and 11-sixteenths.

Just don't tell the wives that it might have been fun.

August 28, 2010

Boozin' buddies toast their friendship

Here's to alcohol: the cause of, and answer to, all of life's problems.
—Homer Simpson

The story should start in a garage. One of those tiny little old ones built to accommodate a Model T and not much else. The shack was behind an old two-storey house Earl was renting not long after getting married. Earl could make wine out of anything. Of course, just because one can make wine out of anything, doesn't mean one should. The batch of crab apple wasn't, strictly speaking, lethal. But in order to drink it, you had to mix it half-and-half with 7Up. Retreating to the garage, ostensibly to fix a toaster, Russ and Earl, young and stupid, were soon sidetracked. The garage had a little wood heater, which meant it had firewood, which meant it contained an axe. What it didn't contain, by the time the evening was done, was a toaster that existed as a three-dimensional object.

Just another episode in a long and blurry relationship between two guys and the liquids they tend to consume when they get together. A cautionary tale, children. Don't do as they do. Don't even do as they say; the words are so slurred you wouldn't understand them anyway.

It started in high school, to tell the truth. Let's not pretend to be shocked. They're not the first underage drinkers ever to learn a lesson, and they won't be the last. Fittingly though, the lesson was taught by a bottle of Teacher's Scotch whisky. You know the message has sunk in when the mere sight of a Teacher's ad ripped from *Maclean's* magazine and taped to your locker is enough to bring back the nausea days later.

It was never about the booze, of course. You don't need that horrible stuff to have a good time. It was about fellowship, fixing small appliances – and games of skill. In the era of under-dash car stereos, double LPs and terry cloth shorts, there was "beersbee." Russ and Earl held the patent on beersbee at one time. Played only on hot summer days, the game of beersbee consisted of tossing a Frisbee at your opponent's empty beer bottle on the ground some distance away. If you knocked it over, he had to have a chug from the not-empty one in his hand. Variation: sit around and drink beer.

If I were naming chapters, I'd call the next one Root Beer Glove Box. Before the proliferation of brewing stores, Russ attempted to learn how to make beer. He started with what he called Pail Ale. It smelled up the whole house but, inexplicably, Russ's parents looked the other way. Perhaps they were relieved that his dalliance with homemade firecrackers had passed.

Around the same time, Earl mentioned the Hires Root Beer kit. You mixed the concentrated flavouring with water to make your own pop. Brewmaster Russ, busy by day getting low-70s in chemistry class, immediately saw the possibilities of adding Fleischmann's baking yeast to the mixture and allowing it to ferment. Then, all you had to do was bottle it, take a couple of bottles over to Earl's for tasting, forget a couple more in his van's glove box and wait for the first warm spring day when the bottles would explode, leaving poor Earl to clean up a sticky, soggy, smelly mess.

Russ's career as a brewmaster peaked with a recipe he found called "Goat Scrotum Ale." The flavourings were juniper berries and spruce needles. Even Earl, who approves of everything homemade merely on principle, declared it to be swill. "Worst beer I ever drank," he said. Russ liked that comment so much he used it on the labels.

Forgiveness is important in a relationship. It's the same with booze – you have to overlook its flaws. Perhaps the most flawed of alcoholic beverages is swish. In the early 1980s, people started buying old whisky barrels to turn into planters. But the ones that came fresh from the distillery had one more job to do first. You'd tip the barrel on its side, pour in a gallon or so of water and rotate the barrel every few days for a couple of weeks. The water soaked the residual whisky out of the charred oak, leaving you with swish. This was the equivalent of licking ashtrays when you ran out of cigarettes. Raw, harsh and mean, swish was one of the few drinks that actually gave you a hangover while you drank it.

Some people say they have a musical soundtrack for their lives. Russ and Earl have a boozetrack. Swish defined their early post-high school era. It went with everything from playing darts in your parents' basement to. . . . Actually, that's all Russ can remember about swish.

The story should end in a 1963 Grand Prix, unrestored, parked for the winter in yet another garage. Sitting on the driver's side is the owner, Russ, now middle-aged. You-know-who's riding shotgun. Did I mention it's the early afternoon of Christmas Eve? And they're both plastered? Don't worry, they're not going anywhere. There isn't even a battery in the car. But there is a box of Christmas booze on-board, the entire supply for the holidays.

Russ and Earl are up to their snouts in it. It no doubt started with an innocent toast to the season and continued with a general sampling of everything from cinnamon schnapps to cheap gin.

They say it's not the destination but the journey. And here in this car going nowhere are two guys, old enough to know better, cutting loose, laughing uproariously and feeling good about being bad. They know they'll have to step out of the car and walk a straight line soon enough. But not quite yet. Somewhere on the road ahead there's a toaster that needs fixing.

March 6, 2010

40: It's the new 30! (You wish)

Lordy, lordy, the indignity of 40. This one is different. Twenty barely registered. Thirty was a breeze (because I thought I was 30 the entire day of my 29th birthday so when the real thing came along it was like I'd already been there). But 40? I can't even spell 40. Is it "fourty" or "forty"? I've got 48 hours to find out.

This is one of those Flamingo Birthdays, isn't it? One where tacky plastic birds magically appear on your front lawn – penguins or, more fittingly, buzzards.

Forty is the new 30, they say. And tofu is the new porterhouse. Forty is such a landmark that there's a special section in the classified ads where newly ordained 40-year-olds are teased, taunted and tortured by their poetic friends.

> Roses are red
> Violets are blue
> A shade over 40
> Is a ghastly hue

Invariably, they've dug up an old photo where the birthday boy is drunk and dressed in women's clothing. Nothing says "I've pretty much given up" like a snapshot of a shirtless guy in a wig holding a beer bottle.

Heck, I'm so old I remember stubby beer bottles. I'm so old that my earliest memories are in black and white. I can almost vividly remember the Apollo 11 moon landing. I was severely shushed for making too much noise while the family gathered around the TV set to watch Neil Armstrong walk on the moon. The picture was blurry, and the sound was scratchy. It was the worst movie I'd ever seen.

I'm so old that I can remember when *Here Come the Seventies* was a new TV show. When I was young, Mr. Dressup's Tickle Trunk wasn't even full yet. I'm ancient enough to remember when pop bottle caps had cork liners and Five Star whisky had actual plastic stars on the bottle to play with. To what end, I now wonder? To pretend you were the sheriff of Drunktown?

I'm not over the hill yet, but I can see it from here. So goes the Hallmark humour. From my vantage point, there was no better view than the one you got while reclining on the rear parcel shelf of the family sedan. Seatbelts being an unproven new technology, this was one of the best places to ride down the highway when you were a child in the '60s. Then the news came out that some kid had died of carbon monoxide poisoning back there. From then on, my parents insisted I either sit on someone's lap or stand on the driveshaft hump – for safety, you know.

Regrets, I've had a few. I missed the entire firecracker era. They were banned by the time I was old enough to pretend I was old enough to buy them. What a rip. To deny a child the thrill of buying Lady Fingers and Block Busters at the corner confectionery – and the power to blow up anything or anyone he felt like – seems rather draconian in retrospect. Thank goodness caps and cap guns were still legal. I'd be a dangerous person today if I hadn't gotten all that shooting out of my system.

There's nothing like a big, fat, round-number birthday to make you take stock of things. What have I accomplished so far? I successfully courted a beautiful girl. Not bad. We had two kids who don't, necessarily, drive us nuts all the time. (But they're not allowed to play with cap guns, so look out.)

On the other hand, I've never climbed Mount Everest; or won the lottery; or caught a really, really big fish; or owned a motorcycle. And time is running out. Imagine: John Lennon got only 40 years. There are people I grew up with who aren't around anymore. Why them? Where am I on the Big Board Game?

On the other, other hand, I now have ear hairs. Ear hairs! I'll be hitching my pants up to my chest before long. Need proof that you're running out of gas? Notice the complete and utter indifference that you now receive from 20-year-old cashier girls at gas bars. Over the hill doesn't even describe it. You're a blob of protoplasm holding a wallet. If I only had that motorcycle . . .

May 24, 2003

You're in trouble in the men's room

An old joke: two men are at the urinals in a public washroom. One zips up and starts to leave. The other man says, "At Yale, they taught us to wash our hands." The first man replies, "At Harvard, they taught us not to pee on them."

I was reminded of that side-splitter the other night. I was at a banquet – a private function, you might say. After the meal, I retired to the lavatory to powder my nose. It was there that I encountered my worst public toilet nightmare: an even number of urinals. There they were, four in a row. Not a problem in an empty bathroom, but in this case there was one guy at Urinal #1 and another at Urinal #4.

Naturally, there was an empty urinal to the right of the first man and to the left of the second. I could have used either. This was not the problem. The problem was, which one to choose.

The First Law of Guyland: One must never pee beside another man if at all possible. A simple edict, but one devilishly difficult to obey in certain circumstances. Like the one I was then facing. If there had been five urinals, things would have been fine. I'd have instinctively chosen the middle one, leaving a safe porcelain buffer on either side of me. If there had been three, no problemo; you have no choice but to sidle up beside the guys already there. Nothing personal, dudes, I'm just doing my business. But no. In this case you have to pick which guy to stand beside. Depending on how fast you walk into a public washroom, you have between one and three seconds to make this crucial decision. Talk about pressure.

I suppose you could stand there and wait to see which fellow finished first. Or chicken out completely and pick a toilet stall. But that might be rude.

Like, "Are you saying you don't want to pee beside me? You're being a little uppity, aren't you? You think you're better than me?"

No, that's just asking for trouble. We're supposed to be men. We don't care where, how or with whom we pee. Heck, the more the merrier. Except that's not true at all. We do care. We just don't care to admit it.

Unfortunately, the pee-position decision is hampered by the Second Law of Guyland: Never look at other guys in a men's room. Entire conversations take place at urinals with guys looking straight ahead, as if the brick wall three inches from their noses is the most fascinating thing they've ever seen. This is normal, acceptable behaviour. What else are you going to do, glance over? What if you saw something? What if the other guy thought you were looking even if you weren't? You'd be crazy to take that chance.

What you're left with is simple, blind intuition – a guess, really.

I blame the problem on the inventors of the individual, free-standing urinal. These were no doubt hailed as a great improvement over the old-fashioned urinal trough. But at least at a trough, no one (one hopes) stands out. You don't have to worry about choosing a spot because everyone is in the same boat, so to speak. Of course, you're slightly more exposed that way, but the law prevails: you don't show me yours and I won't show you mine.

The simple act of public peeing is far more complex than it should be. No one teaches you the right way to do it. Like, where does one aim? Directly into the delightfully named "urinal cake"? Straight ahead? Straight up? Which tactic results in the least splashing? You can't exactly ask the guy next to you which way he prefers.

And what about the egregious lack of common courtesy that plays out all too often around the urinal? Like, what kind of moron spits his chewing gum down there? I can only hope the janitorial industry has specially designed pincers for removing such foreign objects. And what about the inconsiderate smoker? What on earth is your butt doing in the urinal? These must be the same guys who practise the art of urinal graffiti. Limited only by the sharpness of their wit and crayons, these Shakespeares and Longfellows come up with such inspired sayings as "(Expletive) U" and "Why are you looking up here, are you ashamed?" Invariably, someone else adds a witty rejoinder like, "No, (expletive) U." The restaurant industry finally put an end to this unpleasantness by installing chalkboards and "captive audience" advertisements above the urinals. Now the vandals are limited only by the sharpness of their pocket knives.

And what of this word "urinal"? I've used it 15 times in this column and cringed every time. It's probably Latin in origin. Every slightly embarrassing word seems to be Latin – from algorithm to vulva. Even innocuous words sound sinister in Latin. (Like "innocuous" and "sinister.") American coins have *E. PLURIBUS UNUM* on them, which means "out of many, one." Sure. Now kindly get ye pluribus away from me.

But back to my initial quandary: where to spend my penny. I don't know what made me do it, but I picked the spot beside the guy on my left. It was a huge gamble. What if the other guy finished first? What if he finished first and then left and then some other guy came in to see me elbow to elbow with my new pee buddy?

Thankfully, the Roman god Urinus was smiling down on me; I guessed correctly! As soon as I pulled up to the American Standard, the guy beside me zipped up and started to walk out. I was, truly, relieved.

"At Yale . . ." I called after him.

February 7, 2004

The great moustache storm has passed

Well, thank goodness that's over. Movember, I mean. I'm sure it was fun for all the guys who last shaved on Halloween and embarked on 30 days of whiskers-gone-wild.

By now, their faces are baby-bottom smooth again, they're splashing water on their chins in slow motion, and they're ready to star in any number of Gillette commercials.

But what's an already-moustachioed man to do? He's not a Movember member, just an outsider looking in at all the fun as everyone from the announcers on TSN to the athletes they report on go from clean-shaven to unclean-shaven.

Oh, and don't they all look rather pleased with themselves, like they've just time travelled and been awarded bit parts on *Magnum P.I.*

But what about those of us who have invested in the whole hairy upper lip thing 24 hours a day and seven days a week? We have an honest, committed relationship with our face foliage. It's not some one-month stand, some tawdry fur-fling.

Not many people know this, but Movember is an extremely awkward time for guys like me who already have a manstache. A couple of weeks ago at lunch, the subject of Movember came up. Every woman at the table agreed that moustaches were uniformly horrible.

They were horrible on strange men. And they were particularly horrible on their own men. Horrible, horrible, horrible.

They agreed, to a woman, that they could not wait for their men to shave the preposterous things off.

And there I sat feeling so self-conscious and humiliated that I had to hide my old-growth lip-forest behind a sandwich. But I was hungry and my cover was soon blown.

In the flurry of 'stache bashing, there was no consideration shown to me. No, "Oops, sorry, Cam. Forgot you had one." Not even a bologna sandwich of a lie like, "Except yours, Cam. Yours looks great."

Maybe they're so used to seeing my moustache that they've forgotten I have one. It's become an invisistache. If that's the case, I have to wonder: what's the point of having one? Wait a second. What *is* the point of having one? It can't be vanity, since it apparently makes me look even worse. It serves no useful purpose, other than as inspiration for creative metaphors. My 'stache, for example, isn't bushy enough to be called a "cookie duster." Even if it were, I doubt it would actually dust cookies. I mean, if your cookies are dusty you should probably be using a Swiffer on them.

Nor is it a soup strainer. But who eats strained soup, anyway? The lumps are the best part – the broth just keeps them warm. Lady tickler? Let's not go there. Now that I realize my moustache doesn't do anything and has no esthetic value, I have to wonder what it's doing there at all. Where, indeed, did it come from?

I think it started as the upper deck of a goatee, which I grew a decade ago to accessorize a Halloween costume. I wanted to look hideous and figured my psycho-killer outfit wasn't scary enough with my other prop: a beef liver skewered on a meat hook.

The best you could say for it? It made me look like I might, someday, own a motorcycle. So Halloween came and went but the goatee stayed, like one of those nuisance party guests. Later, I booted the chin part out and cleaned up the rest into whatever it is that I have now.

And there it sits. It doesn't do much. Evidently, it doesn't raise eyebrows. It certainly doesn't raise money. I should probably just shave it off. But not right now. The nation's sinks are already clogged with whiskers. I think I'll wait until Furbruary.

December 3, 2011

Get less out of life: ride a one-speed bicycle

I think I might have a problem. It's possible that I've become a bike hoarder. I now have (ahem) five rideable bikes. One more and I'll be a bicycle cat lady.

Bike to Work Day is coming up. As I take inventory of my fleet, I don't know which to choose. I have three one-speeds. One, I keep at work. I call it the 24-Hour News Cycle. I am so funny. I have one three-speed. And I have one bike with 18-speeds (or something) that I rescued from rusty-chain hell. My last ride on it had a certain poetic symmetry – the trip was to buy pedals.

Gears are fine, but I'm starting to question the more-is-better thing in cycling. And, perhaps, life.

I recognize the advantages of multiple gears. When you go uphill, you can downshift so it's not so hard. And you can really give 'er going downhill. Shifting to the biggest sprocket in the front and the smallest sprocket in the back, you can cover about three city blocks with one rotation of the pedals.

I should be amazed by multi-geared bikes but by now they're just a useful tool to me. Maybe it's because I have an irrational aversion to the word "derailleur." That's the spring-loaded lever-and-sprocket thing in the back that nudges the chain back and forth. Derailleur: hard to spell, impossible to pronounce. Only people in the Tour de France should be allowed to use words like derailleur.

What really turns my crank these days are one-speed bikes, particularly relics from the '70s when everything didn't have to be so complicated. With the momentum of the world relentlessly driving toward more and bigger, a one-speed bike might be more than a one-speed bike.

Can people get by with fewer speeds? Fewer complications? I wonder. The trend in home building is to tear down a small house and build a mansion in its place. There's one under construction just a few pedal strokes from my place. It looks like a boutique hotel. It's tragically hilarious. I predict there will eventually be two Audis in the driveway, each with an eight-speed transmission. To live that kind of life, you need all eight. But nine would be better.

One-speed bikes are different. You are immediately aware of their limitations and you have no option but to adjust to them. Try going downhill really fast and your knees fly up and down like pistons and your legs turn into a blur and you picture the horrible cartwheeling crash of an experimental aircraft. "SHE'S BREAKING UP! SHE'S BREAKING UP!" Yeah, no. Don't do that. At the very least, you look ridiculous. When you reach terminal velocity on a one-speed, all you can do is coast. That's fine. You need balance in your life: some work, some rest. When you do stop pedalling, a miracle happens. You have time to look around, to smell the air, to enjoy the scenery. On an 18-speed, you can just keep pedalling, much like a big mortgage keeps you working.

Sometimes life is smooth and flat. And sometimes it's uphill. With a one-speed, you have no choice but to work harder. Stand on the pedals. Grit your teeth. Gut it out. It will make you stronger. But what if the hill is too steep? Gosh, you might have to get off your bike and walk. "What?" you say. "Me? Walk? But I'm busy and important. I can't be expected to walk – I'm late for a meeting at the bank to finance my chipboard Taj Mahal!" One-speeds instill a smidge of humility. They slow you down, inside and out. Can you learn more about yourself when you don't have everything you could possibly want? I think so. One-speeds remind me a bit of camping – you go out of your way to live a version of your life with less stuff to rely on. Makes you feel good. Puts things in perspective.

Of course, it's possible to pitch your tent beside an air-conditioned fifth-wheel camper with central vac and a generator that makes you want to turn into Charles Manson. Some people will always think more is more. I'd like to say they're wrong. But did I mention I have five bikes?

June 19, 2015

Stop drinking, but save some room for cake

"Your future is in your hand," the talking urinal cake said. No, that's not the opening line of my new novel. It's the latest innovation in the war against drunk driving.

Various U.S. states have employed talking urinal cakes in tavern toilets to influence men to be aware of the dangers of driving under the influence. "We want to turn some heads," said Michael L. Prince, director of the Michigan Office of Highway Safety Planning. OK, Mike, I'll make the jokes around here.

The facts are sobering, the statistics arresting: men are three times more likely to drive drunk than women. And 98 times more likely to use a urinal before they do. So they stagger into the restroom, unzip, let loose, sigh, and then hear a woman's voice talking to them. This is what she says: "Listen up. That's right, I'm talking to you. Had a few drinks? Maybe a few too many? Then do yourself and everyone else a favour: call a sober friend or a cab. Oh, and don't forget to wash your hands."

It's an instant attention grabber, likely because it's the first time a woman has talked to the dude all night. As a bonus for the state, some guys will think they're hearing things and swear off drinking altogether. But cynics will resent the encroachment on their personal space during such an intimate moment. Out of spite, they will ignore the message. This is what you would call a backlash. (Not the same as a backsplash, note.)

Now that we're in the age of talking urinal cakes, it's only a matter of time before your pee station is programmed to broadcast all sorts of things. Sardonic laughter, for instance. That will sober a guy up right quick. Or friendly reminders:

"Are these your sunglasses?"

"This is not a chewing gum receptacle."

"Um, have you seen your doctor lately? Just asking."

If urinal cakes drown out the guy next to you, I'm all for them. There is a certain kind of guy who can't stand the minute of awkward silence that ensues when one is busy spending his penny. He'll do anything to break the tension – whistle, hum, clear his throat – while you're staring at the wall and trying to think about Niagara Falls and overflowing eavestroughs. Count yourself lucky if this is all he does. Other guys will poke through the tension by – gasp! – trying to talk to you.

"Drizzling again, eh?"

"What? Oh, the weather, yeah." Or: "You don't buy beer, you only rent it!"

"Yes! That is funny! I have never heard that one before!"

Considering how long men have been going No. 1, there have been precious few urinal innovations over the years, particularly on the blank wall above the urinal. Men did what they could to help by carving messages there with their jackknives. It took a few hundred years, but bar owners finally wised up and installed blackboards. Men could write whatever they wanted with chalk. Men responded by carving messages on the blackboard with their jackknives.

Store advertising followed, posters encased in clear plastic. Invariably, they were fancy ads for menswear. Each and every one featured an angry, leggy supermodel glaring at a nicely dressed guy who is sitting on the hood of his Lamborghini, staring vacantly toward the horizon. The message: God, it's depressing being rich and stylish. As far as in-pee entertainment went, fashion posters were only marginally better than reading the plumbing itself: Crane Presto. American Standard. "Patented in 1958? Well, that's something."

Fancy restaurants are now spending millions installing individual TVs in front of urinals. They all show soccer, to make sure no one stays too long. One place has a soothing voice reading books. P.D. James is popular.

All this care and attention, and we still haven't found a way to avoid using the term "urinal cake." Now those are two words you don't want in the same sentence. Urinal cake. It's the kind of term that's hard to forget, that tends to hang in the air. The person who invented the term "urinal cake" clearly had no respect for cake. Couldn't they have called it a "urinal disc," and got on with their business?

At any rate, talking urinal cakes (icing not included) cost $21 each and last three months. Few are expected to be stolen.

July 8, 2012

Chapter 7

Nostalgiaholic

I can't believe you made it this far. No, I shouldn't say that. Of course you made it this far. You have excellent taste. I think you will find this chapter appealing. Perhaps bittersweet, with subtle notes of vanilla and blackberries. I'm rather partial to it. In fact, the other chapters should thank me for keeping them in the book.

I happen to be a nostalgiaholic. I've looked back fondly on the good old days since about Grade 3. Here's my childhood in a nutshell: Riding my bike to the store for candy in the summer. Counting the days until the Exhibition. Jumping into a pile of crisp poplar leaves in the fall. Counting the days until Halloween. Wearing lace-up moccasins all winter. Taking the bus downtown on a Saturday to shop for plastic model kits at Handicraft Supplies. Tobogganing. And counting the days until Christmas. *It was great.*

Some kids I knew couldn't wait to grow up. I was in no particular hurry because I was having a good time. When I was eight, my parents went berry picking up north. That was not my favourite. I usually waited in the car. But one afternoon, we stopped in at Zeden Lake for a swim. There was a high wooden platform in the water. You climbed it and jumped. It was more exciting than anything I could imagine. I remember appreciating the appreciation of it. That can't be normal. I willed myself to never forget it, and I never have.

The squish of warm back-alley mud between the toes. Scrounging pop bottles to play pinball at the candy store if the big kids weren't there. Outdoor swimming lessons in a freezing pool. Fries and gravy at The Bay cafeteria. And never a parent to be seen. Memory mining: it's where the gold is.

We lived half a block from the elementary school. Going home for lunch was nothing special. The treat was bringing a sandwich and staying over the lunch hour. I made my own chocolate milk with cocoa and sugar and put it in a mason jar; the glass Thermos liner was always broken.

We lived in a bus-route bungalow. Two parents, six kids. I was the youngest. I remember, when I was quite small, my mother telling a friend that I was the "bonus baby." Took me 20 years to figure that out. Wait a second . . .

When my mom died, I said this in her eulogy:

> *I don't remember my mom complaining once about having six kids. If anything, she took the struggles as a point of pride. I was oblivious to the sacrifices it took. I thought that fried potatoes were best when you added bread cubes.*
>
> *But love is priceless, and we were rich. One day around Grade 4, I was walking home with a buddy who surprised me by saying he was jealous. He lived in a bigger house, and he had all the model kits that I wanted. He was jealous, he said, because my mom didn't call me "Cam." She called me "Love." I'd heard it so often that it didn't register. But it did after that. When I was bad, she called me something else: Cam Joseph Stinkpot Fuller. Stinkpot!*
>
> *My mom couldn't remember a punchline to save her life, but she had a colourful lexicon: "Conniption." "By cracky." "Cripes all fishhooks." Good children were "little ticks." Bad ones were "little rotters." If you wanted to clean something, all it took was a little elbow grease. A little hard work never hurt anyone. You might as well save your breath to cool your soup. I won't mention her many inventive uses of the S-word.*

My mother was a voracious reader – almost exclusively of fiction. "Don't you read non-fiction?" I asked her in her last year. "No," she said. "There's already too much non-fiction in my life."

I inherited my mom's love of language and put it to work. If she liked one of my columns, she clipped it out. The other ones, she didn't say much about.

"What did you think of *that* one?" I would ask.

She'd turn her head like a toddler refusing mashed peas and say, "Not my favourite."

The pivotal moment of my childhood was finding out that people thought I was funny. I remember the instant it happened. One night after supper when I was in Grade 2 or 3, two of my teenaged brothers were squaring off in a nasty verbal sparring match. I could feel the tension in the room building, and I didn't like it.

"Get off my back!" one of my brothers yelled. Yikes, this was getting serious.

Impersonating John Wayne from some flea-bitten Western, I lowered my voice an octave and intoned, "Yeah, dis . . . mount!"

It wasn't much of a joke, I know. But you have to understand how adorable I was. Everyone in the kitchen cracked up. The tension was defused. *I did that.* It was like finding out you could look through walls or lift a car. I was hooked. I became the family quipster.

Now that I think of it, most of my column-writing career has been devoted to chasing that first laugh. Even so, I hesitate to go back there too often. I fret that it makes me sound 90 years old. "The good old days." Such a cliché. But sometimes you just want to smell the inside of a snow tunnel again, to feel the side-aching church giggles, to ride your bike fast enough to scare yourself. That's what being a nostalgiaholic is all about.

At recess, anyone could lose their marbles

Every year, when spring rolled around, kids would start playing marbles.

Maybe kids still play marbles. But I doubt it, because you have to go outside to play marbles and I haven't seen a kid outside playing anything since 1987.

Not true. Now that I think of it, some kids played road hockey on my street one day this winter. I should have snapped a photo to prove it really happened, like a Loch Ness Monster sighting.

I hated to have to drive by them to get to my house. I was worried they would get discouraged and stop playing road hockey forever. Kids aren't as resilient as they used to be, you know. And I was right. I never saw them again, the whole winter.

So let's assume kids don't play marbles anymore. Man, are they missing out. Marbles were the best. THE BEST. This was partly because playing marbles was one of the first things kids did after the snow was gone. The sun was finally warm and you could start smelling mud and green grass again. The world felt like a gift. You didn't know what you'd done to be so lucky.

Kids didn't even play marbles the right way, and it was still huge. A game of real marbles was horribly complicated. You had to draw a circle in the dirt and . . . that's just it. Only two kids in 20 knew what to do next. Sometimes you did see kids playing real marbles but you usually felt sorry for them because it looked like something kids would have done in the 1950s – and when you thought of things from the 1950s, you pictured the *See Spot Run* books where the boys had brush cuts and crisply ironed button-up short sleeve shirts and nerd bikes AND REALLY BORING LIVES.

But you were cooler because when you played marbles, you played "hit 'em, you get 'em." This was great. Half the kids were like carnies in their game booths. The other half were suckers.

The rules were both simple and indefinite, if that's even possible. A kid would sit and line up a few marbles in the playing triangle formed by his outstretched legs. He'd place a few marbles in a row. He decided how many marbles, and of what type, and how much space was between each. Then another kid with marbles would come along and try to hit the lined-up marbles with his marbles – from a distance determined by the kid running the operation. The contestant got to keep the ones he hit. The operator kept the ones that missed, often amassing bulging pockets of marbles by the end of the day. This is how casinos got started.

Marbles taught you about life. Some kids were rich, some were poor. Some were reckless, some were cautious. Some were greedy, some generous.

Like kids, not all marbles were equal. Everybody had the cheap cat-eye ones. But what you really wanted were "crystals." They didn't have anything in the middle of them, just more glass. They were miraculous. There were rumours you could actually buy crystals at a store called the Rock Shop but no parent was ever going to drive you there.

And then some kid would come along who not only had crystals but the beyond-rare super-large crystals. How the heck? And then you'd find out the kid's mom bought them for him. Instantly, envy changed to pity. Any kid who got crystals from his parents instead of winning them honestly on the pavement was spoiled. Spoiled kids were reviled. Sorry, but that's just the way it was.

And then there were steelies. Technically, they were ball bearings and not marbles at all, but a steelie the size of a Ping-Pong ball was spectacular because it weighed about a million pounds.

One day, some kid gave me a steelie. Just gave it to me. It was the best thing I'd ever owned. I couldn't wait to get it home. Then I promptly lost it during recess. It fell through a hole in my pocket. That's another thing kids don't have anymore – holes in their pockets.

I scoured the playground through misty eyes looking in vain for the lost steelie. I was so upset I didn't hear the bell, and the teacher had to come out and find me. The defeat! The humiliation!

Sadly, that wasn't the last time I lost my marbles.

May 1, 2015

When a kid takes the wheel, childhood speeds by

Back when the rocks were still cooling on Earth, many families had a car that didn't matter.

Maybe it was an old car replaced by a new one but kept around because it was too crappy to trade in. But for some reason or other, there was always a semi-obsolete sedan just hanging around.

For children of the era, the cars were giant-sized toys with steering wheels that really steered the wheels and windows that really rolled down. We were drawn to them, as if the musky scent of grease and sun-baked vinyl were addictive. Well, time speeds by. Eventually, kids who could never reach the pedals could reach the pedals.

Uh-oh. By one's early teens, a shiny new dilemma came rolling off the assembly line. You weren't old enough to drive a car. Not even close. But you were old enough to WANT to drive a car. And so temptation did what it does. Let us examine one particular case, that of a young man of 13 or so, bored to death on a beautiful Saturday afternoon in the fall.

The parents were out shopping for groceries or buying Danish furniture. And the keys of the car that didn't matter were hanging up on the kitchen pegboard. Any harm in going out there and playing the radio?

My, what a slippery slope. The novelty of the radio wore off quickly, replaced by illicit curiosity: would the car start? The mere thought unleashed a hoard of butterflies in the stomach.

Might as well just turn the key and see what would happen. And what would happen would be this: an alarming ka-junka ka-junka ka-junka as the car lurched forward like an animal being prodded in the flank.

It was in gear. Enough adventure for one day. Time to hang the key back up and recover from the heart attack.

But the dance with danger had begun. Impossible to stop thinking about it now. Of course! The clutch pedal had to be pressed down before turning the key. And you already knew the shift pattern from observing the sequence from the back seat a million times.

Soon enough, idle hands would visit the devil's workshop. When the coast was clear, there was time for some driveway driving. Clutch down, key turned, first gear, clutch up ever so slowly, give 'er some gas. The buzz of the motor, the reluctant whine of the gearbox saying, "What do you think you're doing?" Motion. Amazing, miraculous motion. Back and forth a few more times. More butterflies. Many more.

Retreat to the house, breathless. Dalliance turned to obsession. One day, the car is parked in front of the house, gathering leaves from the poplar. It might as well have winked and given you a come-hither finger. It was time.

Maybe I'll just sit in it. Maybe I'll just see if it starts. One lie followed another. Maybe I'll put it in gear and drive a couple of inches.

Suddenly, you're driving down the street. Regret hits immediately, head-on. "What a stupid idea!" It felt so wrong to be driving – exactly as wrong as it was exciting. Despite all the misgivings, this was true: all the childhood ways of getting around, all the bikes, all the go-karts, all the toboggans – all were instantly devalued. They would never be the same, never as good as this.

Sadly this story, being a true story, contains the fatal flaw of nothing happening. The cops don't pull the car over. A snoopy neighbour doesn't phone the parents to squeal. No pets get run over. The kid simply makes four right turns and arrives in front of the house where it all started. The perfect crime.

Relief. Exhilaration. Pride. Guilt. And then life's revenge: it would be three years before you could drive legally. And now you knew how great it was! The only saving grace: 16 years old in the mirror is closer than it appears.

October 14, 2016

Four vintage 'toys' that nearly brought my young life to an end

Looking back, it's a miracle I survived my own childhood.

In the car, it was a time when parents vented their cigarette smoke by rolling down the window half an inch. Oh, and seatbelts? What are you, a wimp?

On the street, it was bikes. Mine was a hand-me-down three-speed with one speed and no brakes. If you needed to slow down, you planned ahead. Oh, and bike helmets? What are you, a wimp? But maybe the most dangerous things around were toys that weren't toys – twigs that were boats, straws that were guns, balloons that were firecrackers. Insulated by innocence, we had no idea how close we were to injury or death.

Toy threat 1: gutter canal

Back then, we had snow in winter and when spring came it all melted in three days. That created a swift current of runoff that rushed down the street to the storm sewer. One year, long before we were born, some kid noticed a dried leaf in the gutter juking and jiving down the road. He imagined it was a boat. He followed it, mesmerized, until it dropped into a subterranean river. A tradition was born.

Subsequent generations of kids did the same thing. It didn't matter what the vessel was – a twig, a pine needle, a toothpick. (Everybody had toothpicks back then because everybody had cavities.) There was riveting tension and suspense watching the boat work its way around pebbles and parked cars until it met its Niagara-sewer-grate fate. Why didn't kids use actual toy boats? Because that would have been too literal; it would have taken the poetry out of it.

Risk assessment: Traffic alert – kids playing on or near road. Grievous bodily injury alert – kid could blind himself by sticking toothpicks in his eyes for absolutely no reason.

Danger rating: Red

Toy threat 2: bike-spoke noisemaker

Back then, discarded cigarette packages weren't hard to find because the ground was pretty much paved with them. It's not that smokers were litterbugs; they liked to help kids make their bikes more interesting. Kids would take a couple of clothespins – also ubiquitous – and affix the cardboard to their bike frames so that it got hit by the spokes as the wheel turned and made a clicking sound. This turned even a routine Popsicle run into something marginally more interesting. (Note: Some kids used playing cards, but our dad needed his for gambling.)

Risk assessment: Exposure to tobacco packaging. Additional hazard – distracted bike riding. Kid looking down to see if his clothespins were still in place might veer into the path of a fuel-tanker truck causing a collision with a bread truck. Result – they'd all be toast.

Danger rating: Red, with tinges of orange, yellow and blue.

Toy threat 3: dart tipped with deadly curare

Not really. It was a pea shooter, really just a glorified drinking straw that shot pebbles or navy beans. It was a low-calibre weapon but uncanny accuracy made it the bane of house cats everywhere.

Risk assessment: High probability of blinding playmate. Cruelty to animals. Self-harm alert – kid might suck instead of blow (again, for absolutely no reason) resulting in asphyxiation. Heimlich manoeuvre not yet popularized.

Danger rating: Really quite red.

Toy threat 4: recycled balloons

You didn't run across balloons all the time, not like today when parents have bags and bags of balloons, all colour coded and sorted for each occasion. Balloons were special, so when they popped after touching the dry, prickly grass (because no one had underground sprinklers), you didn't just throw the rubber remains in the garbage. With some practice and excellent sucking power, you could make a mini-balloon inside your mouth. Then you could rub it against your teeth to make an excruciatingly annoying squeaking noise. After that, you could bite down on it to make it pop inside your mouth to see how much it hurt.

Risk assessment: Latex allergy alert. Choking alert. Eye and hearing protection required.

Danger rating: Red. And blue and yellow and green and white.

April 15, 2016

Back then, kids were tough – and stupid

"Father," I imagine my children saying. "Life must have been terribly exciting in the winter when you were small. Tell us a story. Pleeese?" I have to imagine my children saying this because, frankly, they're not much interested. But I don't mind making up imaginary children who think I'm fascinating. In fact, while I'm at it, I think I'll give them adorable English accents. "Winta." "Fah-tha." "Smoll." Aah. That's betta.

And so, after they fetch my slippers and sit at my feet, I light my pipe(?!) and indulge their insatiable curiosity. In winter, children of my generation had a certain taste for danger. A game wasn't truly fun unless you could seriously hurt yourself. The means to this end entailed sliding, falling and burning.

Sliding

Tough kids were poor kids, and poor kids couldn't afford bus fare so they invented bumper shining.

Several conditions had to be met before bumper shining was possible. First, it had to be cold out. Brass-monkey cold. Ice-fog cold. Tongue-stuck cold. You also needed footwear without much traction. But this happened to be the age of mukluks. Not the fancy fur ones but plain grey horsehide utilitarian ones. The uppers, which laced up through metal eyelets, were rough, kind of like suede. But the bottoms were smooth leather. You could slide down a hill with them if you were too tough to use a toboggan.

And you could bumper shine in them. Bumper shining. You'd hide near a bus stop. When the bus stopped, you'd wait for the precise moment when it started moving again. Then you'd run after it, latch on to the rear bumper and get a free ride. Oh, the illicit thrill: snowy road speeding by under your feet, wind in your tuque, pedestrians looking on in admiration. Bumper shining. Has ever a name been so perfectly conceived? Has ever a childhood diversion ever been as completely and utterly nuts? What if you mistimed it and slid under the back wheel of the bus? What if you got run over by the car behind you – and back then, believe me, cars were way heavier. Crazy, I tell you.

I assume that not one of these dire consequences occurred to any bumper shiner, ever. On the other hand, it's possible that they did, and that kids bumper shined anyway. Now that's tough.

Falling

Falling is fun and exciting. It's like flying, in a way, if you don't count the impact. Falling is the reason kids line up for the diving board at the pool and ride their bikes down hills. But in the winter, you have to find other ways to fall. Tobogganing is a kind of controlled falling. But for real falling, you had to jump off of something.

I couldn't imagine any kid being luckier than I was that a neighbour's garage was right next to our backyard patio. By shovelling off the patio and surrounding bits of yard, you could accumulate a nice big pile of snow. Then it was a simple matter of climbing the fence, wriggling onto the garage roof, launching yourself skyward and then plummeting to the snow pile below. If it wasn't too hard, it wouldn't knock your wind out and cause cranial bleeding. I still have a photo of my buddy in mid-air, executing a forward flip and about to land smack on his back. Falling is fun.

Burning

Let's say, hypothetically, that the two youngest children in the family are home alone with their grandfather who is making an infrequent visit from the farm and is supposed to be babysitting. He wears wool pants with cuffs. When he lights his pipe and blows out the wooden match, he puts the wooden match into the cuff of his pants.

He's old. Everything about him is old. His car is old. He has tufts of ear hair. The wrinkles on his forehead move up and down when he chews. Being old, he doesn't have much use for babysitting. Truth be told, children kind of sour his milk. He also doesn't have much use for stairs. So you and your sister know you can do pretty much anything in the basement. And in this case, "pretty much anything" means playing with the space heater.

The space heater is really neat because it's like a big dish with spirals of wires in the middle that glow red. Curious children being curious children, you wonder if those red-hot wires could catch anything on fire. Hmmm.

Believe it or not, drinking straws weren't always plastic. In fact, they started out as paper. If a straw spent too long in your mouth, the end would get soggy and collapse and you'd need another one – which you wouldn't get because that would be extravagant. Paper straws, adults would tell you, didn't grow on trees. Which, now that you think of it, isn't true at all.

But straws weren't always just for drinking. Sometimes, they were used in science experiments. But first you had to sneak upstairs and casually grab a few from the tea towel drawer without arousing the suspicions of the ancient farmer asleep in the chair in the living room. Easy.

Now, to put the hypothesis to the test. Touch straw to glowing red coils. After a dramatic pause, a satisfying poof and then fascinating, mysterious, dangerous fire. Blow out fire. Light straw again to verify the results. Blow out fire. With no smoke detectors in the house, it could go on for hours. THIS IS SO COOL.

Honestly, it's a bloody miracle we survived childhood. "And that, dear children, is how we had fun in the winter time."

"Zzzzzzzz."

"Children? Children? Just as well. Do as I say, not as I did. The guardian angels were exhausted and on stress leave long before you came along."

December 14, 2014

Getting to the root of scary basements

What is it about basements? Why are they so scary? Other parts of the house need decorations to be scary. A front yard isn't scary unless you add fake graves and yellow caution tape. Bathrooms aren't scary, usually. It depends on who was in there before you, of course.

But basements are under the ground. The whole groaning weight of the house is above your head. There's only one way out. If you're going to be chased by a malevolent spirit, it's going to happen in a basement. And it's going to be dark, and you're going to trip trying to run up the stairs and you're going to get dragged back down.

In a world of scary basements, the basement at my grandma and grandpa's house was the scariest. The wooden stairs were creaky and steep. It was poorly lit. Once you were down there, it was a long way back to the kitchen. If you had to run for help, there was no way you were going to make it.

There were two main areas in the basement. The worst one was the "root cellar." They didn't say "root," though. They said "ruht." It was a rhut cellar. "Stop saying rhut, it's root!" I wanted to scream, but, of course, I couldn't because I was five.

Even the word "cellar" bothered me. It was an old word from the black-and-white days. No one said cellar anymore, only grandparents who didn't know better and old aunts with wrinkly stockings the colour of lunch bags. I did not like old aunts. They lived in houses you never saw and when they came to visit they knew who you were even if you didn't know who they were, and they pinched your cheeks.

Cellars weren't good. Scary movies had cellars. That's where Vincent Price tortured people.

I knew what a rhut cellar was. It was where the dead vegetables went. I was a city kid and we never had a garden. The idea of storing large amounts of vegetables in the dark and dirt for months on end was beyond alarming. What was a root cellar but a potato graveyard? I was too young to be sent down there for dead carrots or dead beets, which is just as well because I knew that if I reached into the cold blackness beyond the cardboard-insulated door, the only thing I would touch would be a skeleton hand.

The second-worst part of the basement was a bedroom that was never used. It seems ridiculous even now that a bedroom would be down there. Why not just pitch a tent in the graveyard on Halloween? The bed had a metal frame of black round tubing. You didn't even want to touch that bed. There was something of the hospital or prison about it.

On the wall there was a large framed photograph of a lady. "That's Auntie So-and-So," they said, as if you were supposed to know. Did she move away? Die? You didn't even want to look at her. No one came down here. Her face looked into an empty room, day and night. A face with eyes that never closed in a basement with a root cellar that was dark all the time? It's no wonder kids have nightmares. It's the sensible thing to do.

We didn't have a cellar. We had a modern house. Our basement had a modern name. It was a "rumpus room." It's where we had our rumpuses. It was a good place, mostly. You didn't want to go into the Aunt Alice room, of course. It was haunted. There was no Aunt Alice, in reality, but when my brother started the rumour that she came up through the crack in the floor of the furnace room, it all made perfect sense. That's why the floor is cracked!

Basements are the scariest part of any house. But closets are also bad. The more you thought about what might be in a closet, the more likely it was that something really was in there. The fear caught its own tail.

Can you see a closet from where you are right now? Is there someone in it? Are you sure? It might be a good idea to hide right now. I don't recommend the basement.

October 27, 2013

What I want to do on my summer vacation

If you could extract DNA from words, this would be my genetic code. It's all here. It's a column with a beginning but no middle or end, a slideshow of little me in the summer. In a way, there's nothing to it – a shimmering leaf on a tree; the roots go without saying. And it ends abruptly, like childhood.

Today, I stand on the glorious brink of three weeks of R and R.

This year, I plan to get my life in order and repair the cracks in my foundation. I am not speaking in philosophical terms here. Our house needs its foundation reparged. Rest and Reparging. And you wonder why Saskatoon is magic.

Obviously, three weeks from now there will be little point offering you one of those horrible essays entitled, "What I did on my summer vacation." That's why this column is called, "What I want to do on my summer vacation."

My ambitions are modest, my budget non-existent. I want to go to places I've already been and do things I've already done. I want to feel what I felt and think what I thought. And I plan to do all this just by remembering.

I want to spend one glorious summer morning looking up and down the back alley for pop bottles. I want to take them to Bill's Confectionery and cash them in. I want to spend 25 cents on the pinball machine in the corner. Actually, it's not a pinball machine. It's an old mechanical baseball game where you pick your pitch (curve, fastball, slider) and try to hit a big ball bearing over the fence. I want to play five games at a nickel each. I want to save a dime or 12 cents or whatever it is and buy a bottle of Mountain Dew to take home. I want to sit on my bike in front of my house and spend an hour or so nursing that pop until the last gulp is as warm and flat as tea.

I want to go to Redberry Lake and put my tender little feet on the blistering hot sand and cry until my dad has to carry me to the blanket.

I want to go back to the summer Kent McDonald and I lied about our age so we could ride the float instead of walk in the Children's Day Parade dressed as two of the 101 Dalmatians.

I want to go to the Knights of Columbus Strawberry Festival at the old clubhouse on Spadina Crescent. I want to sit in the cool hall on a cold metal stacking chair and watch ancient Abbott and Costello films. I want to line up for a curious square of dry sponge cake and the big scoop of ice cream and strawberries that make it palatable.

I want to go to the Exhibition and sit on the tailgate of the family station wagon and get scared again by the fireworks and have my brothers and sisters try to console me.

I want to take the bus downtown to Handicraft Supplies on a rainy Saturday and spend about two hours drooling over $10 airplanes before buying a $2.50 one.

I want to get a real plastic boomerang and actually make it return. I want to plan my day around watching a rerun of *Mission Impossible*. I want to buy a new package of clear plastic tips for my Duncan Spin Top.

I want Mom to send me to the IGA to buy McGavin's hamburger buns (sweet as candy floss), delectable meat patties called Steakettes, Kingsford briquettes and a box of Fudgsicles. No doubt about it: barbecue tonight. Yahoo!

Just as the summer starts getting routine, I want to find out we're going to the lake for a few days. This will set off a furious shopping spree for the essentials: inflatable toys, swim mask and fins. There will be in-depth comparison shopping between Woolworth's and The Met, the latter winning the contract on the sale price of their Scooby Doo air mattress. On the day we leave, I want to blow my allowance on comic books and Hot Rods for the long ride up north.

I want to go back to that day we went swimming at Zeden Lake when Guy, the oldest, and me, the youngest, spent a couple of hours jumping off a diving tower that looked as high as the Bessborough. That was the only summer I remember my age. "You are eight," I said to myself. "This is great. Remember this. You are eight."

June 15, 1996

When pain was fun, fun was painful

Back in the '70s, torture was a legitimate form of expression among children.

Hence the Bumps. The lucky birthday kid would be cornered at recess, thrown to the ground and have his legs and arms grabbed by the surrounding crowd. He was tossed into the air and then dropped, ever so gently, for every year of his life. When it was over, but before the kid had a chance to compose himself, he'd probably also get a "pinch to grow an inch" and other forms of bonus pain. I forget what they were called. "A punch to finish your lunch?" "A scratch to match the batch?" It was acceptable as long as it rhymed.

The Bumps ended when you got too heavy, fortunately, which allowed you to have more birthdays. It's odd but the birthday kid felt special getting the Bumps. They made you the centre of attention. Far worse to be ignored. As they say, "the only bad publicity is no publicity."

As the youngest of six, I was treated to more than my share of torture in the '70s. There's an old family photo from my grandparents' 50th anniversary party. I'm on my back on the lawn, all wild blond hair (hair!) and skinny arms. The reason I am on my back is because my brother has me pinned down. He's looking at me, but I'm grinning at the camera and making a muscle with one free arm. It's surprising I'm smiling because the position of our bodies suggests that I am about to be subjected to the dreaded Spit Torture. I'm pretty sure my brother invented it. If not, he studied at the feet of the masters.

In Spit Torture, the torturer pins you down, snorts up a mouthful of mucous and then lets it ooze through his pursed lips directly above your face. The skilled practitioner would let the slime droop, until just before the breaking point, then suck it back up. Don't be put off by the description. It's even grosser than it sounds.

Looking back, one wonders why kids didn't yell and scream and call for mom. That's the curious thing about torture in the '70s – parents never intervened. Kids were left to their own devices. They had to learn to protect themselves. It instilled independence. That's what I tell myself, anyway. I hope the truth isn't something less noble, that the moms and dads and uncles and aunts who could have helped were simply too busy in the house pouring rye and sevens and smoking their faces off.

Logic had no place in torture in the '70s. The Snake Bite had nothing to do with snakes or bites. This torment began when someone bigger than you would say, "Give me your arm." Naturally, you would. That's just what you did. The sadistic sibling would then grasp your forearm with both hands and twist the skin in opposite directions, as if they were wringing out a wash rag. But it wasn't a wash rag. It was your arm. And it hurt. And the next time someone said, "Give me your arm"? You would.

Some tortures might not even have a name. There was one with a belt. The heartless psychopath, or "brother," would take a thick leather belt, fold it in half and hold both ends. You would be invited to put your hand in the gap in the middle. The torturer would then pull on both ends of the belt simultaneously, stinging your hand in the middle.

In the '70s, we didn't need to see TV heroes pulling wires out of lamps and electrocuting suspects to know that common household items could be fashioned into torture instruments. Take the simple tea towel. It made a perfect whip when you were drying dishes. (Experts knew to wet the corner to make it more painful when it hit the butt.) Retaliation followed. Inevitably, the whips would be aimed higher and higher. The loser was the one blinded first. "Don't make me come over there," your dad said, lighting another Rothmans.

Looking back, it's amazing anyone lived surrounded by so much pain. The Charley Horse (Punching someone in that sweet spot in the middle thigh was great for getting your place back when you were watching TV.), the Wet Willie (What was worse, the headlock or the cold saliva in your ear? Are you kidding? It was the cold saliva in your ear!), and all manner of nipple pinching, underwear pulling and kick-me-sign posting that kept classmates, brothers and sisters humble and let them know that, in a bizarre way, they were loved. Loved to death.

Aaah, the good old days. In a bout of nostalgia, I took off my belt yesterday and ordered my son to put his hand in the middle. He refused. I couldn't believe it. Kids today. No sense of tradition. He's just begging for a Pink Belly.

March 28, 2009

Helicopter parents keep kids grounded

Parenting then and now is a question of perception. And go-karts. Yesterday's parents didn't know what that noise was in the basement, all that sawing and pounding. They were just glad you were keeping busy. Today's parents would insist on airbags and anti-lock brakes.

I'm glad I grew up when I did. There were no parents hovering above me when I built my go-kart. No one asked why I needed a power drill. No one intervened when I used a butcher knife to cut the rope for the steering system. It wasn't "Don't run with that knife, young man." It was "Point the blade down when you run with that knife, young man."

No one measured the volatile organic compounds in the paint I needed for the super-cool P-40-style shark mouth on the vehicle's front. And no one questioned the absence of any kind of safety equipment that would inhibit motive force. "Brakes," in other words. Didn't have any.

What would a kid's plan be for stopping his go-kart without brakes? There were three options:

1. Bail out at the last minute. It wasn't practical, but the mere thought of it conjured up exciting stuntman highlights from *The Rockford Files* and *Cannon*.

2. Feet. The application of rubber sneaker bottoms to the concrete sidewalk as it blurred by might suffice. Hey – it worked for Fred and Barney.

3. The Veer. The veer was your best option. Braking efficiency varied by season, therefore. You had less stopping power in the early spring before the lawns thickened up and quite a bit later on when the grass was mid-summer lush. Too bad you couldn't choose when you needed to stop.

Despite the danger, I had no peers who were killed or injured in runaway go-kart incidents. But that was before we could instantly learn about every bad thing happening to every kid everywhere in the world. Terror overload has made childhood seem a very dangerous place. The aerospace industry has responded by ramping up production of helicopter parents, hovering over their precious little Fontleroys and Belindas lest they pick up a sliver from their eco-friendly bamboo building blocks.

A helicopter parent would have spent a lot of time around me because I had a fondness for climbing. I apprenticed on fences and earned my journeyman papers on a huge poplar tree in the front yard. One day, my buddy and I got into a whole case of Coke. It was incredibly exotic because it was canned Coke that came from out-of-province. We spent the afternoon climbing the tree and decorating it with empty Coke cans. We were perfect perpetual motion machines; the energy expended in the effort of climbing was replaced in 12-ounce jolts.

No nutritionist was called to the scene of the crime. No one wondered where that boy's mother was. It was summer. Everybody knew where she was – in the kitchen making potato salad. Had I plummeted to the ground, a twitching mess of caffeine and sugar, no one would have faulted her inattention. We're talking potato salad here.

As I surveyed my kingdom, there wasn't a rooftop that didn't beckon. Jumping off the backyard shed was great for entertaining friends. Those faint of heart could use a tree branch to break their fall. If they missed, they learned a valuable lesson: the difference between what you think you can do and what you can actually do. Still, it's just as well we didn't own an umbrella.

Climbing ability was currency. The better you were, the more fun you could buy. Those who could shimmy onto the roof of the school deserved to be there. It was our Everest – with the added benefit of toys on top: lost-forever Frisbees and red rubber balls. The school was surrounded by houses. And we were up there in the broad daylight. But no one ever called the cops. Somehow, that would have been rude.

Today, we concern ourselves with banning Kinder Surprises because some kid might choke on the toy inside. Here's an idea: don't eat the toy. They say that if you don't know yourself, you have no identity. How is a kid going to gain a strong sense of self without knowing how many jawbreakers he can cram into his mouth? We thwart a kid's sense of adventure and then curse him for having no imagination. How are you going to learn what happens when you stuff your mouth full of potato chips and cream soda without actually trying it?

If the classic spring and summer toy, the balsa wood airplane, is a metaphor for childhood, here's the difference between yesterday's parents and today's parents: Yesterday's parents looked at the wings. Today's parents look at the landing gear.

Personally, I lived for balsa airplanes. Gliders were cool. But once in a while you acquired a propeller-equipped model. I had one that showed particular promise. One summer evening after supper (potato salad!) I received special permission to launch it from the roof of the house.

With the family gathered below, I wound the rubber band just enough and released the plane at just the right angle. It caught a perfect breeze, banked left and silently soared in wide, elegant circles, high above its backyard airfield – an epic, once-in-a-lifetime flight. Free and unfettered, it soared. We soared.

May 14, 2011

Ain't no cure for the suppertime blues

As a kid, I remember asking, "What's for supper?" and really, really caring about the answer.

Supper could make or break your whole day. If it was something you liked, there was jubilation. Something you hated was cause for great sadness. I now realize it was less about food than power. When you're the kid, you have no control. You didn't buy the food, you're not cooking the food. You're invited only because it would be against the law for them not to provide you with the necessities of life. And by "necessities of life," I don't mean liver and onions.

When the answer to the question, "What's for supper?" was "Liver and onions," there wasn't just great sadness but great despair. In the mind of a child, nothing justified liver and onions. Not, "But your father loves liver and onions," or "We haven't had liver and onions in ages," or "You'd like it if you tried it" or any other adult-centric excuse. Liver and onions simply wasn't food. NO FAIR! Thank goodness for mashed potatoes and bacon. That's what my mother always made with liver and onions. So liver and onions night was actually mashed potatoes and bacon night. Thanks to ketchup, you managed to survive, but barely.

And yet, one of my brothers actually liked liver and onions. Even at five, I sensed the betrayal, the damage this did to our solidarity. They could exploit this weakness, turn us against each other. They knew a house divided (by organ meat) cannot stand. And I had a sister who absolutely loved chicken livers. Chicken livers? What kind of people am I related to? Sorry, but I prefer to eat chicken from the outside-in rather than the inside-out.

Sad suppers change over the years. I used to hate brussels sprouts – hate them! – but now I like them. They would have contributed to a sad supper then, but they wouldn't now. Ditto cabbage rolls – fine today, bad back then. As a kid, a cabbage roll was just a rice delivery system. You really can't expect kids to like sewage-treatment-plant vegetables like brussels sprouts and cabbage. Children's taste buds are too sensitive. It takes years of adult coffee drinking to dull them down. That probably explains the liver and onions thing. People who start their day with a cigarette in the bathroom probably think they're eating filet mignon and coquilles Saint-Jacques.

What makes supper a sad supper? Try adding breakfast food to it. When I was about 10, I used to help my mother go door to door canvassing for charity. When doors opened and the suppertime smell of fried eggs wafted out, it made me feel sad inside, like we should be giving *them* money. Eggs for supper is a truly sad supper. It's a supper that says, "There's nothing else in the house," a supper that's waiting for its luck to change, for the cheque to arrive in the mail. It's a supper that never had a chance. And don't try to hide it by fancying up the eggs – cheese omelette, Denver sandwich (Why were they always grey?) – they're still eggs and they're still in the wrong neighbourhood.

Pancakes? Not for supper, please, even on Mardi Gras, a.k.a. Fat Tuesday. According to tradition, you're supposed to eat all the good things in the house on the day before the start of Lent, to remove the temptation for the next 40 days of self-denial. Man, if the best thing you have in the house is pancake mix and syrup, you're living Lent year-round.

Lunch food makes for sad suppers as well. I love canned beans, but not after 1 p.m. Here's a sad supper that didn't have to be sad: hamburger patties (so far so good, nothing wrong with that, would've been better with hamburger buns but nobody's perfect) and (ouch!) canned beans. Things were going so well there before the can opener came out.

I will concede that one person's sad supper is another's happy supper. When tuna casserole comes up in the rotation, I admit, I cry inwardly a little. Cry, and plot to sneak out to McDonald's later in the evening – even when I'm the one who's cooked the offending casserole. I never do make the secret burger trip, but the conspiracy gets me through the first few bites. Tuna casserole. Sigh. Tuna casserole would be so much better if you replaced the tuna with rib steak and the noodles with baked potatoes.

"What's for supper?" Now that I have kids, I get asked the question. Every day. The oven mitt is on the other hand. I now appreciate what my poor mother was up against – and she had three times as many ingrates to nourish. And this was decades before the invention of McCain Superfries.

Cooking something everyone can agree on is like lining up a culinary Rubik's Cube. Only two things get the colours to match: spaghetti and chili. But you can't make those every week. What you really want to try is moussaka, but the sight of eggplant might trigger a mutiny.

Yet, one day, sick of playing it safe, you find the courage and put jambalaya in front of them. And they love it! Those are the happy-supper moments the parent-chef lives for. You're so proud of the kids for keeping an open mind. And relieved. Because little did anyone know that if jambalaya didn't work out, it was fried egg sandwiches for everyone. Harsh? Hardly. Wait till I get my mother's recipe for creamed onions.

January 23, 2010

What if I got sick of classic rock?

I had this horrible question pop into my head the other day. I was driving back to work from lunch. I turned the car radio on to preset 2. The song was *Bohemian Rhapsody* by Queen. I quickly changed stations. You can't mess with *Bohemian Rhapsody*. Either you commit to it and are willing to have it going through your head for the rest of the day: "Bismillah! We will not let you go, let him go. Bismillah! We will not let you go, let me go." Or you get the hell out of its way, and fast.

Preset 6 was playing *The Joker* by the Steve Miller Band. "Some people call me Maurice (wee-woo!) 'Cause I speak of the pompatus of love." Bismillah? Pompatus? Magnificent. It's like the legends had their own special language.

But I'd heard *The Joker* a lot recently, and it wasn't doing it for me, so I poked preset 3 on my radio with almost enough force to sprain my index finger. That station was playing a staple of Canadian radio from the 1980s, *Never Said I Loved You* by the Payolas with guest singer Carole Pope of Rough Trade. Such an odd song it is, with a Caribbean beat that no one asked for and Carole Pope's stiff, jagged, palsied talk-singing.

"Never said I loved you. 'Cause I didn't want to lower my guard." It was a revelation looking up those lyrics just now. After a billion listens, I thought the words were "Never said I loved you. Didn't know I'm a god." What's really weird is that I never once doubted those were the actual words.

To recap, three songs I've known for eons were playing on three stations at the same time and the only thing I wanted to do was turn the radio off. Uh-oh.

What if I was getting sick of classic rock?

What if I wake up one morning and don't care who they are – you know, the boys in the bright white sports car? Or where they got that car? What a horrible thought. I was raised on classic rock. But back then, you know, it was just called rock. When *Hot Blooded* by Foreigner came on the radio, you turned it up, not off.

Way back when I ripped the AM radio out of the dash of my car and got my first good stereo, the first song I heard on the first FM station I tried was *Tom Sawyer* by Rush. I didn't even like Rush. But when you've shoehorned 6x9 speakers into your Corolla, let me tell you, *Tom Sawyer* rocks whether you like Rush or not. I've liked *Tom Sawyer* ever since. I'll have to read the book someday.

That's how classic rock works. It puts an imaginary electrode in your brain and pokes the very same synapses that fired the first time – back when you were young and cool and at the high school dance, say, and *Bad Case of Loving You* by Robert Palmer came on and there was an actual girl in front of you, and the entire world was perfect.

I like to imagine it's been the same way through the centuries, that something similar happened to Beethoven's brain when he listened to a rockin'

Bach fugue and noticed a girl across the room who had the same hair as Farrah Fawcett.

But what kind of world would it be if classic rock didn't work the same magic that it used to? I suspect it's walking a fine line between popularity and self-destruction. This made me wonder if there's a mythological creature that actually eats itself, so I looked it up and sure enough there is – the fearsome Ouroboros. It looks exactly like Jon Bon Jovi.

I'm scared now. What if *Don't Stop Believin'* comes on when I'm alone in the garage and I don't feel like doing an elaborate fist-pull-down when the Journey guy wails, "Hiding . . . somewhere in the NI-EE-IGHT!!!"

Oh, it's too sad to contemplate. Imagine a world where *Tonite Is a Wonderful Time to Fall in Love* doesn't make your head bob, where the most potent April Wine hits have no effect on you whatsoever.

The alternative? I suppose I could look for songs that were written after 1979, but I'm too old to find out what's cool and get all into it. Basia Bulat? What if I pronounce her name wrong? What if I spell Timber Timbre Timbre Timber? The kids would laugh at me, that's what. I'd end up looking like an old fool – not like I do when *Jump* comes on the car radio and I play air synth.

Oh, Van Halen. We'll dance, dance, dance the night away.

November 16, 2014

Chapter 8

But Seriously, Folks

Real newspaper columnists, following the footsteps of the angry, sweaty men who came before them, prefer to be feared. They don't like to talk about how great it feels when somebody actually *likes* something they did. But the truth is, it's absolutely fantastic.

The first column I ever wrote, a little thing called "A bad case of video shock," came out on December 18, 1991. Terribly dated now, it's about trying to find a good movie in the video store. The deafening roar of crickets heralded its arrival.

My second column, "Film blabbers spoil movie for everyone else," had a longer shelf life. I took a lifetime of frustration out on people who talk during movies. A few days after the item ran, I was out for supper with my future wife when the server told me how great he thought my movie-talker column was. I couldn't believe it. Positive feedback from someone who wasn't my mother!

A lot of things rush through a columnist's mind in moments like that – all of them, strangely, in italics.

What? He read it? And liked it? But how did he know who I was? Of course! The picture with the column! I wonder which part he liked the best. I should ask. No, that would be stupid. Don't look so needy. Just play it cool, man. Say thanks and change the subject.

The waiter's compliment certainly didn't hurt his tip, I'll tell you that.

Hey! Maybe that's why he was buttering me up?

No! Don't spoil this for me!

Columnists of great substance, on the other hand, probably get stopped on the street all the time by fans saying stuff like, "Excellent point about the UN Security Council!" An elderly man once stopped *me* on the street. I thought he was going to yell at me for riding my bike on the sidewalk. But no. "How do you make those garlic mashed potatoes?" he asked.

I thought he was off his rocker until I remembered having written about garlic mashed potatoes some months before.

I outlasted about five publishers in my career. I remember only one of them complimenting me on a column. It was the one I wrote about how men choose which urinal to use. Who needs to write about world peace when potatoes and pee get you that kind of attention?

Writing about yourself is a tricky thing to do. No one is going to care about your problems unless they can identify with them. Failing that, it's best to make sure you're the butt of the joke. (Speaking of which, I should get around to that colonoscopy column.) I did write about getting a CAT scan once. "Computed Tomography can give multiple views of organs such as the pancreas, liver and Hammond b-3," I wrote. *Parum pum.*

I got my sense of humour from my dad, but, unlike me, he never tried too hard to get a laugh. When my dad died, I agonized over whether I should write a column about him. It couldn't be sappy, that's for sure. I came up with "Goodbye is all we've got left to say." I stole the title from a Steve Earle song.

The column you worry about most is the next one. What will it be about? Where will the idea come from? You're always looking for ideas, weighing their merits. You kind of hover above yourself like a bee looking for pollen. Thoughts that may become columns one day are scribbled in shorthand on the backs of envelopes and scraps of paper. Sometimes an excellent idea dies on the vine. Sometimes, you take an average idea and it blossoms. Sometimes, you think you've done a brilliant job and nobody says a word. Well, it's better than hearing "not my favourite."

I reckon I've written about 1,000 columns over 25 years. It's been an incredible privilege to crack a few jokes and maybe break the tension in your life and mine a time or two. I can only hope the laughs were genuine – and any insights worthwhile.

How one little thing can trigger
an avalanche of memories

A storage room is a distant galaxy, a place where time and space are malleable.

In this particular storage room, one of the objects in orbit is a white kiddie table and two chairs.

The tabletop is covered with snapshots of two small children. The film – and it was film – fixed them forever in moments of time with cousins and uncles, aunts and grandparents. A clear plastic cover protects the display.

It's things like these that basements are full of. The table and chairs haven't been used in years. But were they ever used, really? Of all the many things that toddlers and preschoolers do – drool, cry, fight, run, hop, fall down – the one thing they never have time for is sitting in chairs.

Therefore, the mini-furniture is in mint condition. But it can't be sold because the photos have personalized it. So there it remains, a small link to a past that's expanding continuously in every direction, as mysteriously as the universe.

It's a dangerous thing to look at a collection of photos of people who will never be as they once were. The gravitational pull of melancholy is a strong one.

It must be noted that he didn't go to the storage room to look at the table and chairs at all, but merely chanced a glance when he was down there – with the expected result.

How on earth did it happen? How did two tiny, bath-fresh babies get big enough to sit on your knee and wind down from a stressful day of toppling lamps by listening to a chapter or two of *Curious George* and other great works of literature? And how did those perpetual motion machines turn into the men they are now, stubbly of chin and deep of voice? You swear you witnessed the evolution, but the miracle of it circles back to Eden.

It might also be noted that the table and chairs had a wise and lively creator. Looking at the furniture, he is reminded of this in an unexpected way. One chair rests on the other, upside down. The bottom of the seat is therefore visible.

Reflexively, he notes there's no finish coat on the bottom of the seat. No reason for it. Who would ever see it? But he sees it now, and what he can see in the absence of a finish coat are brush marks in the flat white primer. And that's what sets him adrift for a minute.

He recognizes those brush marks as well as any art appraiser would evaluate the ones in a framed masterpiece. He knows them so well that he can actually picture the hand that made them, from the way it held the brush to the manner in which it moved – an assertive swish from left to right and then right to left. It was as clear and detailed as if he were looking over the painter's shoulder.

An illusion? Certainly. But an honest illusion, if there can be such a thing – real and unreal in the same way that the light from a star can reach the earth millions of years after the star itself has shone its last.

He looks again at the brush marks and smiles when he remembers the day it just happens to be: May 5. Of course. And the year IT happened? Of course it doesn't matter. One year later or a million, it would always seem like a second ago: The gathered family, the hushed goodbyes, the unfathomable mystery of space and time.

Back on earth, full of thoughts, he goes upstairs to find a piece of paper. On it he scribbles "0505 brush marks." Might come in handy one day.

May 13, 2016

Trump Effect emboldens haters to spew toxic ideas

On a late fall weekend, city police were forced to shoot a coyote that was threatening people on the riverbank near the University of Saskatchewan campus. It was too bad it had to happen, but the animal had become emboldened and was a threat. He'd been there all summer, stalking people who were walking their dogs.

"Something is going on out here," I thought back in June. On a bike ride, I caught a glimpse of the coyote myself, hiding in the bushes. Let me tell you, the security you take for granted as a city dweller disappears in an instant when you imagine an animal like that coming after you. It's the age-old conflict between nature and society. Incidents like these, rare though they may be, are a sad but inevitable part of urban life. I read the story like everyone else and forgot about it.

Then, on Monday, the city editor of this fine newspaper received a phone call from a person who might have been as disturbed as that poor animal. I hope so, anyway, because if they were serious and believed what they were saying then our city has a bigger problem than a random incident of wild animal encroachment.

The phone call was brief and to the point.

"They should leave the coyotes alone and shoot the immigrants instead," the woman said before hanging up.

There was a chill in the newsroom – fittingly, it was Halloween. Something is going on out there when people like the coyote lady are feeling confident enough to share their toxic thoughts.

Maybe it's the Trump Effect.

Maybe these people would have remained hidden in the bushes if Trump hadn't offered them some twisted sense of empowerment to let their hate flag fly.

But someone is listening to them now. Someone understands them. They're free from their shackles of shame and fear. They've been emboldened, you might say. They've made conflict inevitable between their hateful nature and decent society. Immigrant or not, imagine someone like that coming after you.

Usually, the workday ends and you forget about the loonies. But it was Halloween and getting dark and that particular call continued to haunt me.

"Shoot the immigrants instead."

Lady, do you know what you're saying?

Did anyone in your family tree ever move from one country to another for a better life? Do you wear a poppy? Have you seen film from the day the Russians liberated Auschwitz? Is that the kind of world you want?

But enough of that. It was Halloween, and it was time to give out treats. The usual suspects arrived throughout the evening – kids who looked like mine, growing up in a safe and secure city, old hands at the game of Halloween, feeling entitled to their treats.

Then, later than I would have expected, the bell rang, and I opened the door to two little girls and their older sister.

Minus the princess costumes, they looked exactly like the children you see in news footage from Syria. Maybe this was their first Halloween. What a strange thing it must have been to dress up on a cold night, stop by the houses of strangers and get candy.

They were terribly cute even though their faces were thin and their eyes wary, like eyes that have seen things that can't be unremembered. I put two mini bags of chips into each of their small plastic jack-o-lanterns. We had plenty and the streets were growing quiet.

Like little birds, they turned and skittered back to their mom. Before I closed the door, I heard one of them excitedly say, "Two!" It was the sweetest thing I'd heard all day.

And so to you, coyote lady, I have to ask: Which one of those kids would you shoot first?

November 4, 2016

Ride a bike. Annoy a driver. Rock the world.

There aren't many ways you can fight authority, change society and tone your thighs all at once. In fact, I can think of only one: by riding a bicycle.

It seems like a simple, innocent thing to do, but riding a bike goes against everything our car-loving culture influences – from materialism and the class system to environmental degradation and ill health.

There's always tension between cars and bikes. I used to think it was because drivers don't like bikes getting in their way, don't like having to be careful around them and hate the way bike riders selectively follow the rules of the road. Is a cyclist on a sidewalk a sign of civilization crumbling? It might well be. But since civilization as we know it kind of sucks anyway, maybe that's a good thing.

Riding a bicycle is the single most subversive thing a citizen can do. Bikes don't run on gas, they don't take up much room, practically anyone can operate one, they don't cost much to buy or maintain and they keep you in shape. For prevailing systems of power, for those who benefit from the status quo, that's a huge threat.

The geo-political thing
If more people used bikes more often, they would buy less gasoline, reducing our dependence on foreign oil and giving us one less reason to invade oil-rich

countries, thus saving the world from messy wars and terrorist backlash. This alarming lack of war would take tax dollars away from inventing invisible warplanes and direct it to paying off debt, increasing foreign aid and curing disease.

Unfortunately, fewer people would die by violence and germs, causing the planet's population to increase to the point where it might threaten the world's food supply. On the other hand, the developed world throws away almost as much food as it produces.

Maybe there would be enough to go around if we just used it efficiently.

And maybe there would be even more to eat if we weren't paving parking lots, growing McMansions on farmland and planting malls in the middle of nowhere that you need a car to get to.

But even if it came down to war, a world of cyclists would have long since beaten all the swords into fenders and turned tanks into rototillers. And, practically, war wouldn't work anyway. You can't invade a country on bicycles; everyone would be laughing too hard to shoot each other.

The urban planning thing

If most people used bicycles as much as they could, cities would be built differently. No one wants to pedal for an hour to work and back. People would live closer to their jobs. There would be more small stores instead of a few huge ones, more coffee shops than transmission shops. And it would be quieter. Downtowns would flourish. Underutilized roads would be converted to pedestrian malls. There would be more street performers. Oh God, mimes!

The job thing

Why do people work? Is it fulfilling? Would they be bored if they didn't? Sure. But people also work to make money to pay for the cars that take them to work. This is insane. Only a bicycle can break you out of this vicious cycle.

The health thing

If the rumours are true, exercise is good for you, both mentally and physically. A culture of bicyclists would put fewer demands on the health-care industrial complex. Big Tobacco would wither and die. Big Pharma would wonder where all their medicated customers went. Freed from the crushing expense of funding hospitals, governments would cut taxes. The average worker's take-home pay would increase. People could afford to retire at a younger age and would enjoy longer, healthier and happier senior years. The cruise ship industry would boom. Curling ratings on TV would skyrocket.

The alien revenge thing

We live indoors, if you think about it. Even when we go "outside," we're still on the only planet in our solar system that has breathable air. You wouldn't start your car and leave it running in your living room. That would be nuts. Yet we think nothing of contaminating the only air in the known universe with noxious chemicals and toxic particles.

Sometime in the future when a more advanced society lands on Earth and starts sifting through our rubble, they'll discover what we did to our air and how we turned our beautiful blue marble into a blob of lead. And they'll say something like (I'm translating now, so it might not be accurate) "They did WHAT? Were they nuts? What a bunch of IDIOTS!" It's up to us to prevent that superior, post-apocalyptic future race of cruel alien know-it-alls from having a laugh at our expense and making fun of our spindly legs.

Get on a bike. Fight the power. Feel the freedom. Stay off the sidewalk.

May 12, 2013

When my tree falls, I will definitely hear it

I'm losing an old friend, and I guess you could say that the sadness is bittersweet. Or maybe tart but juicy.

The old friend is the apple tree in the backyard. I don't know how old it is, but it's been there longer than we've owned the house, more than 20 years.

Things seemed fine until this spring, when the tree suddenly wasn't itself. Leaves came out, then died on dying branches. The blossoms gave way to apples, but much fewer than normal. Many of them started to grow, then stopped. The ones left are now falling off. There will be a kind of woody thump as another despairing apple gives up and jumps.

THWUMP. THWUMP. The Reaper knocks on the door.

I know, I know. An apple tree dies every six seconds (a statistic I clearly just made up). But this isn't just an apple tree. It's the best apple tree ever.

It grows full-sized apples like the ones you buy in the store. I grew up with crab-apple trees. Crabs weren't fruit, they were ammunition. You could eat them, I guess. As preserves, they probably tasted great over ice cream. But everything tastes great over ice cream.

The retired couple we bought our house from had a large-scale vegetable grow-op. They had two plum trees, two apple trees, raspberries, strawberries and a huge garden. Their mindset seemed to be that if your dirt wasn't sprouting something that could be frozen, canned or eaten on the spot, it was a waste.

My parents were of the same generation and had the same view. They couldn't stand to see an apple die in vain. To my shock, when they came over to visit the kids, they even picked apples off the ground. The 1930s did strange things to people.

But when my mother started making pies from my apples, it was clear this was no ordinary apple tree. Those pies were fantastic, mysteriously better than pies made from the same kind of apples grown on the same kind of trees.

I was hooked. I quickly developed a pie problem. I became a fall apple peeler and a winter pie baker.

Season after season, the apple tree kept time. Blossoms in May for my birthday. The miracle of free apples growing all summer long. The fall harvest. The endless wait of winter.

Trees and time. When my kids were in Grade 1, I took a picture of them in front of the apple tree on their first day of school. And the year after that, and the year after that.

The series is complete at 12. In the first few photos, the backpack is wearing the kid. In later years, their expressions say, "Hurry up, this is embarrassing." In the final one, the subjects have whiskers. They're mature enough to humour the photographer, but not exactly eager to endorse the tradition.

You wonder how it happened, how your willowy saplings ended up with rough bark. How they grew so fast, got so tall.

And suddenly, it's been ages since your parents dropped by with a five-gallon pail to race the ants to the windfall. Gone so long already.

I guess what surprises me most about my apple tree is how fast it faltered. A year ago, it was groaning under the weight of a bumper crop. I'd never seen it produce so many apples. I could barely keep up with the picking and peeling and freezing. It was a glorious final chapter in a book that didn't have as many pages as you thought it did.

We'll plant another apple tree in the spring, of course. The rest is up to fate. How many harvests will I have with it? When my years run out, who will be the next apple lover to enjoy its spring blossoms and fall bounty? These things can't be known.

Trees and time keep their secrets.

August 7, 2015

Home is where the hearth is

It seems like, oh, about two hours ago that we opened up the family cabin for the summer.

Suddenly, somehow, it's now closed for the winter. How can that happen? How can a season come and go as quick as the flick of a squirrel's tail?

I was there when we opened it at the end of May and I was there when we closed it last weekend. I prefer the opening part. It's all so exciting and new. Winter has been survived. Summer is a promise sure to be kept. The best four long weekends of the season lie ahead: Victoria Day (anticipation), Canada Day (celebration), that wonderfully contrived first-Monday-in-August holiday where you can almost feel the season slipping away and everyone tries to have more fun than they probably should (desperation) and, finally, the unavoidable sadness of Labour Day (resignation).

From the sunny hillside of late spring, however, the view is clear, and the only thing that stands between you and three months of carefree cottaging is 238 kilometres of blacktop, 1,552 camper trailers going 83 kilometres an hour and the damn plumbing.

Yeah, the plumbing. Every year, it's something stupid. We used to get our water directly from the lake, filter it (through old sports socks, I think) and use it for drinking. No one got sick, but we all got tired of having to re-anchor the water line every time the waves got too high. I have fond memories of one of my brothers-in-law, wearing leaky hip waders, freezing parts he didn't know he had, trying to locate the foot valve in three-foot swells. Comic relief aside, it was time for a new system. We finally got a well, which provides us with an endless supply of perfectly safe drinking water that smells kind of funny when it comes out of the hot water tap. As a result, we haul most of our drinking water from home.

We still need the well for washing and flushing, of course. Getting the system up and running every spring has become a bit of a Monty Python skit. Last year, we convinced ourselves the pump was frozen in the well. I spent hours boiling pots of lake water on the stove and pouring it down the well to thaw the phantom ice. Finally, we discovered the reason we had no water pressure: a never-used tap was open in the crawl space under the cabin – and, around it, a quickly growing basement swimming pool.

On opening day this spring, one of my brothers discovered a dead animal in the toilet. He called me up to take a look. It was one of those horror movie cliché moments.

Why is he going into the bathroom alone when the rest of his friends are downstairs???

I took a look in the bowl. I actually heard the music from the *Psycho* shower scene in my head as I looked down and saw a deceased squirrel floating in antifreeze. It looked like a discarded hairbrush, *au jus*.

A few minutes later, this same brother noticed a problem with the kitchen drain. The pipe had frozen and cracked. But why? Because a bat had fallen/flown/crawled down the vent, died and expanded upon freezing. We immediately vowed to put a piece of screen over the vent pipe on the roof. Never got around to it, though.

To tell the truth, we don't get around to much as summer progresses. Everybody is too busy doing nothing to spoil their summer weekends with work. And so time marches on. I'm never so conscious of time as I am at the lake. Every sunset has symbolic meaning. Every fall makes you think about things you don't want to. The place echoes with the sound of minutes ticking into years.

Our cabin goes back 20 years. It all started in 1981. A young Grant Devine was promising to put a hot tub in every driveway. *Saturday Night Live* was still funny. And my parents decided to build a vacation property. We are not wealthy people, but pooling our shares of Grandma and Grandpa's modest estate got us started. That seed money gave the place a sense of history before the first nail was driven.

Over the next couple of years, all six kids and their various spouses helped build our cabin. But most of the work was done by Mom and Dad, sacrificing time and money, devoting countless hours to the place during off-season work bees that the rest of us were hardly aware of. It was something more than a building to them.

Their signature piece is a spectacular stone fireplace, each rock chosen for its unique character. Grandchildren, too young to understand, are duly shown the various features of the fireplace: a fossil here, an interesting shape there. It's a quiet little initiation.

I shouldn't be surprised that one season slipped away so quickly, since the past 20 have done the same thing. The lake looks the same. The leaves change colour and fall to the ground just like they always have. The cabin itself is holding up amazingly well. And the fireplace looks great. But its builders are most definitely 20 years older. You can't get around the math: $55 + 20 = 75$. Throw in a few variables, like ill health and bad luck, and it's a daunting equation.

Middle age has turned into old age in the flick of a squirrel's tail. I don't think my parents would have the strength in their hands to mix the mortar and then muscle the rock of that fireplace into position the way they once did. Thankfully, they built it to last. And suddenly, somehow, their grand-children are old enough to cuddle their own sleeping babies in front of that remarkable fireplace. And when those babies are old enough, we'll teach them what it means.

October 13, 2001

Goodbye is all we've got left to say

A car pulls into a restful place on a cool May morning. A few memories spring to the driver's mind.

He brought home the worst Christmas tree ever. It looked like an abstract drawing of a Christmas tree. All his kids could hope for was that it would fill out once it thawed. An hour later, it looked worse. There are some Christmas trees with a flat side that can stand against a wall. Worse ones need a corner. This one needed two corners. They knew for certain this would be the worst Christmas ever when he got out his power drill and started relocating branches into the bare spots. An older brother saved the day by finding a much better tree. Eventually, they'd all look back on the incident and laugh. Eventually.

∞

He was running the bingo tent at the Exhibition and looking after his youngest of six kids. He told the preschooler that it would be okay to get on the airplane ride as long as the boy told the operator that his dad was a "Carnie." In fact, the father was trying to sneak off and play a couple of hands of blackjack at the casino. When the boy got in line, he realized all the other kids had tickets. He scoured the bottom of that little airplane for one of his own, but in vain. When the ride operator got to him, and he had no ticket, he kicked him off. The kid still remembers running away crying, "My dad's a Carnegie!"

∞

He was a painter for most of his life. Not art but walls. He always seemed to be the oldest guy on the job site, which allowed him to cultivate a crotchety old-geezer persona. They called him "Stormin' Norman." Of the many things he hated, the worst was a radio blaring Top 40 hits while he was trying to work. "You like that better than music?" he'd shout at the drywallers, who never quite got what he meant. Once, he made sure he was the first one on the job and then took a pair of wire cutters to the back of someone's stereo. Stormin' Norman, indeed.

∞

"Sastoon," he said, pushing the brim of his hat up with his thumb. This was in answer to the question, "Where are you folks from?" The questioner was the tow truck driver who was saving a middle-aged couple and their two youngest children from spending the night on the Hanson Lake Road, where their old Dodge sedan had broken down. Maybe it was the effect of the hot sun, or the giddy relief of being rescued, but for whatever reason, the hat-pushing-back gesture and that mispronounced hometown were the most hilarious things those two kids had ever heard in their entire lives. All they had to do to crack each other up for the next year was touch thumb-to-forehead and say in a deep voice, "Sastoon."

∞

He never ended a telephone call by saying "Goodbye." That might have been interpreted as a display of emotion, something that was unpalatable to him. Instead, he simply said what he had to say and left you to conclude that the conversation had ended when you heard the click on the other end of the line. Conversations, therefore, sounded like this:

"You still have my drop sheets?"

"Yeah, I'll bring them over tomorrow."

Pause. Click.

One of his hired men, a cheeky young painter, caught on to this quirk and began saying, "You gonna say goodbye, Norm?" seconds before the inevitable click. It must have worn him down because he mellowed in retirement, and his phone calls started ending with a new, comparatively affectionate and cheerful sign-off. Conversations now sounded like this:

"You still have my drop sheets?"

"Yeah, I'll bring them over tomorrow."

"Very good."

∞

He never spent more than a minute longer than he had to in school, and he disdained books unless they were fact-based; the idea of being swept away by "fiction" was a sign of weakness. Yet, somehow, he was more quotable than most authors. "She ain't the Taj Mahal," he'd say when his workers were being too fussy on a paint job. If you'd spent 10 hours of back-breaking labour, climbing ladders in the hot sun, did he try to console you with, "Oh, you poor thing, you must be exhausted"? No, not him. Instead, it was, "That'll knock the horns off ya." If something smelled, it could be really bad or bad enough to "knock a skunk off a gut wagon." There was only one punishment good enough for chippy hockey players: "Comb his hair with a hockey stick!" He didn't ask if you wanted to play cards, he offered to "give you a cribbage lesson." When he was winning, you were getting an "arse-luffin." When he was losing, he had "good position." And no fishing trip was complete until he said the magic words: "The Queen ain't eating fresh pickerel, boys." You want to catch one now, just to be able to say it.

∞

The new parents needed a gate to keep their kids safe in the yard. He offered to build one. "Can you build it by the end of next month?" they wondered. "I'll build it tomorrow," he declared. And he did.

∞

The ceremony is brief and it's time to leave the cemetery. The driver searches for words but finds only a couple: Very good, Dad. Very good. ·

May 22, 2004

The men's trip finds life in the dying season

The fall men's trip to the cabin is one I anticipate like no other. It's a wonderful weekend of fellowship and food, work and weather.

I remember a few years ago, standing on the deck in the crisp dark with my brother-in-law, son and nephews, looking up in childlike wonder at the stars, thinking, "This could be the best moment of my life." Okay, the glass in my hand might have influenced my opinion, but still.

You can't go to the lake in the fall without being amazed at the transformation from summer. On the water it's achingly quiet, the buzz of boats having faded away weeks before. On land, near and far, chainsaws are going about their pre-winter work as if in a constant rage.

On the trees, lake leaves seem to turn with a fatalistic resignation that you don't see in the city, like prey that knows it's caught and done for. The weather is definitely changing. The wind hides a sharp edge of cold steel behind its back. Fall is the shortest season of the year. It can end suddenly under a white sheet before its work is done. You just never know. The chatter of the drying leaves is like a whisper in your ear: "Our time has come. And you will join us."

It's true. You can't walk through fall, you can't inhale its earthy, spicy scent without thinking unthinkable thoughts about your own mortality. Best to keep busy, which we do. There's firewood to cut, the yard to clean up. The only break is the one you get on the ride to the landfill. Good to be busy. Good to tease and kibitz with the fellows. Good to feel tired. Good to have earned those aches and that first end-of-day beer.

And all the while, like money in the bank, supper has been cooking. It seems logical to choose a manly slab of beef. Five pounds of brisket should do it. The cut was undressed of its brown waxed paper and lovingly massaged with a mixture of brown sugar and enticing spices like coriander, cumin and cinnamon 24 hours before cooking time. Then, about noon on Saturday, it was put into the oven at a mere 300 degrees Fahrenheit.

A warm oven on a fall day is an embrace, it's protection, it's the promise of sustenance. But one must be patient. All afternoon, the blackening spice and rendering fat fill the cabin with a maddeningly enticing aroma. Every trip from the cool outside to the warm inside is a masochist's dream, welcomed torture.

Finally, the meal. The men swarm the roast with primal, monosyllabic exclamations of awe and enjoyment, reckless gustation ending in regretful groans of overindulgence that seem to echo off the pine and cedar walls.

Then maybe, just maybe, if the weather is right and the libations have verged on excess, a gauntlet might be dropped, a feat of strength proposed: a suicide night-swim in the freezing lake. The black, scary lake that might be harbouring the world's biggest northern pike that could take a casual chomp and leave you with the nickname Lefty until the end of your days. The icy cold lake that halts your progress by mid-calf, washing away any memory you might have had that a dip was a good idea. The vast, impassive lake that can only be conquered if you dive in. Because it doesn't count if your hair doesn't get wet.

And so, cursing and thanking the fortifying gulp of rum that sponsored the escapade, you foolishly risk heart failure with one final, season-ending plunge into the abyss. It's an icicle exclamation point on the season. It's a screaming pronouncement to the starry sky that you're alive. It's fall again. And you're alive.

September 23, 2017

Maybe this is how we find out what we're made of

"Can I help?"

If you've ever been asked that question, you know how good it feels. A few years ago, when my job and life stresses were coming together like vinegar and baking soda (yay, chemistry), a friend at work offered those three words. It's likely she doesn't even remember doing it, but it's something I'll never forget.

"Can I help?"

There was comfort in being asked that simple question, and relief, and a hint that I mattered. It's a powerful question. It must be, because the question itself made a difference.

And now the world has embraced Humboldt and is asking the same thing. There are events in life that don't make sense, that won't ever make sense, that are outrageously unfair and unbearably cruel. There are times when fate turns, looks impassively at the vulnerable people it has forced to their knees, and shrugs.

It's too big to fight. There's no winning. You can't put your hand up and stop the wind blowing across a field on a frozen April day when spring and life and lives are postponed, perhaps indefinitely.

And yet, what we've seen in the past few days isn't resignation. It's been a collective, intuitive, immediate and heartfelt effort to make a difference regardless of the odds – countless gestures that speak to the basic decency of people. There's money, of course, a staggering GoFundMe tally that started with a typically humble Saskatchewan goal of $5,000, a fund that includes everything from Halsey Husson's $5 to a CBC reporter's $50 to thousands of dollars from major league teams and players.

"This is how we help . . . for now," said Hayley Wickenheiser, urging donations. Celebrities have used their status to lend moral support. The NHL Jets and Blackhawks replaced their names with Broncos for Saturday night's game. Don Cherry and Ron MacLean were on a plane to Saskatoon as soon as they heard. From more unexpected corners, there was Ellen DeGeneres expressing her sorrow and Prince Philip and the Queen giving thoughts and prayers. I was in the newsroom on Saturday when President

Trump's tweet was noticed. Reporters looked up, a bit wide-eyed, said not much, and got back to work.

Musician and philanthropist Tom Jackson was moved to write a poem. "Mom yells 'Dinner's ready at the hall of fame. Come on before it gets cold, let's watch the game.' " Tom Cochrane was asked about his once again timely highway tragedy song *Big League*. "Out after school, back on ice. That was his life, he was gonna play in the big league." Cochrane performs in Saskatoon this summer. That song will resonate like never before.

Backed by the power of social media, people are encouraging each other to wear Broncos colours. Apparel manufacturers are ramping up production with no thought of profit. The touching #PutYourStickOut campaign on Twitter has inspired thousands, including Canadian Forces personnel in Iraq.

There's no way to change what happened and nobody thinks there is. But maybe our answer to the unfairness is to change ourselves. How much do we take each other for granted on those days when we allow ourselves to be seduced into thinking it'll last forever? How do we treat people we don't know? Is that glare when an insignificant traffic dispute arises entirely necessary? Have I ever thanked the woman who dumps the trash can beside my desk? Do we envy someone who has a "better" life or brush past another who doesn't?

There are reports of surviving players fighting for their lives in hospital. It's all a fight. A fight to believe it actually happened, a fight to understand, a fight to keep going, a fight to make a meaningful contribution.

What is the right thing to do? Everything. "Ring the bells that still can ring, forget your perfect offering. There's a crack in everything, that's how the light gets in." Leonard Cohen. I think he played left wing. We are imperfect. But in times like this we are something more important, which is wonderfully human. Keep it going. Like The Wave in an arena.

Can I help?

April 11, 2018

A fire, a woolly mammoth and, maybe, a lesson

Cam Fuller died on December 19, 2018, at the age of 55. This column was first published on May 26 of that year.

There's a lesson for me in the Kyle Hotel fire. It's just that I'm not sure what it is.

On May 14, I was driving from Medicine Hat to Saskatoon. The middle part is a clear shot from Swift Current to Rosetown on Highway 4, a two-lane stereotype of Saskatchewan-straight pavement made for big pickup trucks to guzzle gallons and spit out miles.

The town of Kyle is on that road. It dates back to 1923, named after original settler Jeremiah Kyle. In the 1960s, they unearthed a 12,000-year-old woolly mammoth while building the highway.

I've passed Kyle quite a few times in my life. In fact, every time in my life. But driving lets you think. What I was thinking on the way down was "Why?" Why don't I ever stop in places like this? Too easy to keep moving. Don't need gas. Plenty of places to eat in Swift or Rosetown, familiar places with familiar food advertised on TV.

But there's something about Saskatchewan's countless Kyles, those faded and peeling places fighting extinction. They had to have been new once; they must have been busy in their day. Between them, you pass farmyards littered with forgotten stories in outdated machinery and classic cars on a journey from dust to dust.

There's always a grand house that's crumbling, a Halloween graveyard, an abandoned motel. What is it about abandoned motels? I picture a person I never was, leaning on a chair in front of a door with a one-digit number on it, rolling a cigarette with one hand and watching the sunset, anxious to get back in the finned Chevy early the next day because, well, there might be a duffel bag stuffed with cash in my trunk.

Back in reality heading home, with the radio on and a big truck in my mirror anxious about passing, I decide that today's the day. I'll stop in Kyle for lunch at that place advertised on a ditch sign. I let the exasperated GMC roar by, find the Farmer's Grill without trying and risk being labelled a troublemaker by opting for the salad instead of french fries. Finally, I'm feeling like the suspicious stranger I wanted to be.

To prolong the fantasy after lunch, I step into the bakery down the street and buy a loaf of white bread, yeasty-fresh and still warm.

And then, I can't even say why, I take a picture of the hotel on the corner – "Suites with kitchens; daily, weekly and monthly rates" – a plain white stucco building with a sign advertising ice for sale, the lettering on the word "ICE" topped with snow. It's Monday, 1:40 p.m.

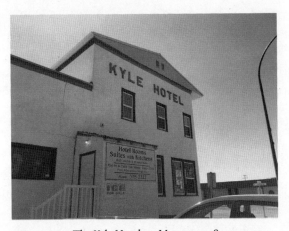

The Kyle Hotel on May 14, 2018

Having scratched whatever itch that was, it was back to numb normalcy heading north. Past the sign for Lacadena, which happens to mean something to me because it's old Fuller territory. Past Elrose. Rosetown seemed positively hectic once I got there. Then it was on to home.

On Wednesday, May 16, at 5:30 p.m. firefighters went down into the basement of the Kyle Hotel, which was full of smoke. They quickly retreated and started spraying water on the buildings nearby. By 8 p.m. the hotel was in ashes, 72 years of history gone in 90 minutes.

Clearly, I'm not the least bit qualified to write about Kyle losing its hotel after seeing it once for two minutes. It's just such an odd thing, having been there and taking what has to be the last picture of it intact, unaware that it had less than 55 hours to live.

It feels like there's a lesson there, if only because I turn 55 today. Maybe it's this: Don't drive by, not every time. Stop for a second. Look around. Take a breath. It's later than you think.

The Kyle Hotel was destroyed by fire on May 16, 2018